inside the BEST SELLERS

inside the BEST SELLERS

JERROLD R. JENKINS WITH MARDI LINK

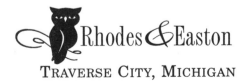
Rhodes & Easton

TRAVERSE CITY, MICHIGAN

 Published by Rhodes &Easton
121 E. Front Street, 4th Floor, Traverse City, Michigan 49684

Publisher's Cataloging-in-Publication Data
Jenkins, Jerrold R.
    Inside the bestsellers : authors reveal their inspiring stories / Jerrold R. Jenkins with Mardi Link. – Traverse City, Mich. :
    Rhodes & Easton, 1997
        p.   ill.   cm.
    Includes bibliographical references and index.
    ISBN: 0-9649401-1-6
    1. Bestsellers–United States–History–20th century. 2 Bestsellers–Authorship.
    3. Self-publishing–United States–History–20th century. I. Link, Mardi. II. Title.
PS169.P64J46 1997
809.04 dc20   96-70375

PROJECT COORDINATED BY JENKINS GROUP, INC.

99   98   97   *   5   4   3   2   1

Printed in the United States of America

*To those aspiring authors
who wish to achieve the same level of success
as the authors between these covers.
– Jerrold R. Jenkins*

*To my Dad, Charles Link, who was privy to most, if not all,
of the wisdom in these bestsellers before they were ever
published. Thanks, Dad, for your advice on life and work.
You were right. I would have made an unhappy veterinarian
but I've become a happy writer.
– Mardi Link*

CONTENTS

FOREWORD   11

PREFACE   13

ACKNOWLEDGMENTS   17

INTRODUCTION   19

Chapter One

The Christmas Box
by Richard Paul Evans   31

Chapter Two

The Celestine Prophecy
by James Redfield   41

Chapter Three

Chicken Soup for the Soul
by Jack Canfield and Mark Victor Hansen   49

Chapter Four

50 Simple Things You Can Do To Save The Earth
by Julie Bennett   61

Chapter Five

1001 Ways to be Romantic
by Greg Godek   67

Chapter Six

Life's Little Instruction Book
by H. Jackson Brown   75

Chapter Seven

Dianetics
by L. Ron Hubbard   83

Chapter Eight

Love You Forever
by Robert Munsch   93

Chapter Nine

The Wealthy Barber
by David Chilton   101

Chapter Ten

When I Am An Old Woman I Shall Wear Purple
Edited by Sandra Haldeman Martz   111

Chapter Eleven

What To Expect When You're Expecting
by Arlene Eisenberg, Heidi Eisenberg Murkoff
and Sandee Eisenberg Hathaway   123

Chapter Twelve

The Macintosh Bible
Edited by Arthur Naiman   131

Chapter Thirteen

The One Minute Manager
by Ken Blanchard 139

Chapter Fourteen

Mutant Message Down Under
by Marlo Morgan 145

Chapter Fifteen

What Color Is Your Parachute?
by Richard Nelson Bolles 153

Chapter Sixteen

Embraced by the Light
by Betty Eadie 161

Chapter Seventeen

How to Keep Your Volkswagen Alive
by John Muir 169

Chapter Eighteen

The Seven Spiritual Laws of Success
by Deepak Chopra 179

Conclusion 187

APPENDIX A 193

APPENDIX B 197

BIBLIOGRAPHY 201

INDEX 203

MARDI LINK 205

ORDER INFORMATION 207

FOREWORD

I had never intended to be a published author, let alone a publisher. *The Christmas Box* was simply a story I wrote for my two daughters to express my love to them.

But by Christmas of 1994, *The Christmas Box* had made history as the first self-published fiction book to make it to *The New York Times Best Seller List.* Suddenly publishers were very interested in my book, and I found that not only did the message of *The Christmas Box* inspire hope, but the journey of *The Christmas Box* inspired hope as well.

Throughout America, and the rest of the world, there were tens of thousands, maybe hundreds of thousands, of writers who wanted to see their book in print. Tired of rejection from publishing houses, writers were pleased that a self-published book was able to break the system — to compete head-on with the multi-million dollar publishers and win. *Chicken Soup for the Soul* was turned down by over thirty publishers. No one would touch *How to Keep Your Volkswagen Alive,* saying there were already enough car repair books on the market. James Redfield, author of *The Celestine Prophecy,* received more than a few rejection letters from publishing companies who were convinced the book would never sell. How then did these rejected

11

manuscripts become best selling books? Each has its own story. And their triumphs are what makes *Inside the Bestsellers* so timely and so valuable.

I remember my frustration after selling more than a quarter of a million copies and having an article turned down by a major magazine because, as they said, "You could not have possibly sold that many books. No one in New York has heard of you." It was my first glimpse into the ethnocentricism of the publishing world. I became acutely aware of this as the New York publishers began calling me for rights to my book.

"Where exactly is Utah?" one asked.

"Somewhere between New York and LA," I replied.

"Well, if you see any other books out there, let us know."

The best-selling, self-published authors in *Inside the Bestsellers* know there is a lot of America between New York and Los Angeles. Though each story is different, there are a few things they all have in common. Each required faith, hope and the energy to work against a system that says you can not succeed.

The success of my book has had a transforming effect on my life and my family's lives, but our story is not the only one. Each author whose story is told within these pages has had their own transforming experience and lived their own success story. Major publishers now frantically scour bookstores and small book shows for self-published books which have the potential of becoming the next *Celestine Prophecy* or *The Christmas Box* . They have opened doors for future best-selling authors that live somewhere in between.

Richard Paul Evans

PREFACE

Just like all of the books profiled in these pages, *Inside the Bestsellers* began with an idea. Actually in this case, it was an idea born out of a certain respect – even awe – I had for other people's ideas. I was struck by what best-selling but previously unknown authors had done with their original ideas, and the way in which their ideas took them to unprecedented places.

In the fall of 1995 I was giving a speech to a group of consultants at a conference in Chicago. I do quite a bit of public speaking, and I've found that it isn't the book sales numbers or the profit dollar amounts or the independent publishing statistics that people in the audience respond to: It's the stories. Start telling your audience stories and the room gets a little quieter, people put down their pens and make eye contact, whispered conversations cease. It's a myth that when children grow up, they outgrow the need to be told stories. Executives and housewives and publishers and even consultants love a good story.

And so I found that the stories behind the millions of books sold and millions of dollars made were what people were interested in. And as a speaker, I found that they could be used in a speech as examples of larger issues.

At this particular conference, I was talking about book ideas and how people had taken ideas and turned them into successful books. It was then that my idea for *Inside the Bestsellers* first came to mind. When you're speaking in front of an audience, that is definitely not the best time to be struck by a potentially life-altering idea. But I wasn't complaining. I thought it was a great idea then, and I still do. I don't think the audience noticed, but for a moment I lost my train of thought; I was so focused on turning the idea into a book.

The following week I gave another speech to another group of consultants, this time in Boston. I told my publishing success stories again, watching the audience carefully for their reaction. Again, they were listening. They were interested. They even asked thoughtful questions and wanted to know more about the authors and their books. But the clincher came after my speech. Several people in the audience approached me in the back of the room, and asked if a book existed that compiled stories of best-selling self-publishers and small publishers. I had to answer no, but assured them that there would be one published soon. This is that book.

About the same time, my company, The Jenkins Group, purchased *Small Press* magazine, a bi-monthly trade journal covering the independent and small press publishing industry. I hired freelance writer and former reporter Mardi Link as managing editor, and shortly thereafter promoted her to executive editor. She was a natural to collaborate with me on the book, taking my notes, ideas, research, contacts and vision and helping to compile the manuscript.

While putting the book together, talking with authors and publishers, researching the history of each book, the stories began to fit together. They formed a trend that has been well-reported within the industry, but all but ignored by the popular media. Publishing as a business is changing. And you as a reader, along with the authors profiled within these pages, are the witnesses to those changes.

I've learned from the very best teacher, experience, that great book ideas cannot be ignored. That despite rejection, ridicule and apathy they have a way of moving forward, of making themselves heard.

Read on. Listen to what these witnesses to a changing industry have to say. But be careful. Your own idea could be formulating right now, just waiting for the perfect moment to appear.

ACKNOWLEDGMENTS

Jerrold R. Jenkins would first like to thank his wife, Julie, and Mardi Link would like to thank her husband, Jay Tomaszewski, for eating dinners alone with the children, respecting the 'Dad's working' and 'Mom's working' signs on our home offices and tip-toeing, whenever possible, while this book was being written.

They would also like to thank the authors for giving wholeheartedly of their time, wisdom and advice on this phenomena we call the best-seller. These 18 writers are the leaders in a continually growing and changing industry which is all the better for their entrance into it.

Thank you to David Hacker, for his careful editing and finally, thank you to the librarians at the Traverse Area District Library, in Traverse City, Michigan, the Northwestern Michigan College Library, also in Traverse City, Michigan and the Central Michigan University library in Mt. Pleasant, Michigan, for their help, patience and interest.

INTRODUCTION

Writing the best-seller: It is a nearly universal aspiration. The desire among bookstore junkies and first-time authors may even be a universal preoccupation. Be honest with yourself. Who among us would say, "No, I don't have a book in me"? And hey, as long as you're snuggling comfortably into your literary daydream, that book may as well put your name right there on the coveted *New York Times* best-seller list.

At one time or another in our lives, most of us have felt the sudden spark of an original idea, and had the impetus to turn it into a book. And why not? In our high-tech, niche-carved, segmented and over-competitive world, writing a bestseller is one of the few remaining ways to get rich quick on your own efforts. But the desire goes beyond material gain. Writing a book that is read by millions is a chance to share your view of the world, to publicly establish your intelligence, sense of humor, gift of drama or expertise. It is a lasting, undeniable blip in eternity's timeline that simply says, "I was here. This is my mark."

Inside The Bestsellers is about writers who did just that, many of them with their first book. But it's about more than

19

just a few authors and how they made it big. All of the books whose stories are told here had small beginnings. They were either self-published, or published by small publishing companies. Many were first rejected by major publishing houses, whose editors didn't find the manuscripts salable. They were either too short or too long; too regional or too broad; too much like another book, or too esoteric. But whatever box was checked on the fill-in-the-blank rejection letters these authors received, if you can make lemonade from lemons, apparently you can also make best-sellers out of the bottom of the slush pile.

Some authors profiled went directly from rejection to self-publishing, wiping out their savings accounts and even borrowing money and going into debt just to print a few thousand books. That's faith. But it's also the 'American Way.' Ignoring the odds, putting your head down and forging ahead despite what fate, or the major publishing houses, throw your way. There's a bit of the pioneer spirit in these writers that would not be denied, and ultimately, is difficult not to admire. And the stories behind their best-sellers are filled with as many plot turns, funny anecdotes and surprise endings as the books they wrote.

Even though the label "best-seller" is almost synonymous with "money-maker," none of the authors interviewed in these pages say they wrote their books for financial gain. Though, make money they did. Richard Paul Evans reportedly received $4.2 million from Simon & Schuster for the hardcover rights to *The Christmas Box* and its prequel, *Timepiece*. Marlo Morgan was paid about $1.7 million from HarperCollins for the rights to *Mutant Message Down Under*. Bantam paid $1.5 million for the paperback rights to Betty Eadie's *Embraced by the Light,* and James Redfield sold the hardcover rights to *The Celestine Prophecy* to Warner Books for $800,000. And all these deals were negotiated by first-time authors!

Those figures surely provide fodder to turn the stories behind each book's success into the future legends of the publishing industry, to be told and re-told like so many fairy tales. Interestingly, in at least one instance, the tide of goodwill towards an author originally seen as being rewarded for a job well done, quickly turned rough and nasty. L. Ron Hubbard, father of the Church of Scientology and author of the mega-seller *Dianetics* once made a flip comment about writing, money and spirituality, that later came back to haunt him.

"Writing for a penny a word is ridiculous," he has been quoted as saying during a speech at a writer's convention in 1949. "If a man really wants to make a million dollars, the best way would be to start his own religion." Despite that oft-quoted remark, Hubbard consistently disputed those who viewed *Dianetics* as a simple con to make the author rich. And, some of the other best-selling authors whose work is profiled in these pages speak of the money generated by their ideas as secondary to the ideas themselves. On the contrary, for writers like Morgan (*Mutant Message Down Under*), Redfield (*The Celestine Prophecy*), and Evans (*The Christmas Box*) the money may actually be counterproductive.

"I'm a visionary writer, and all the high-profile stuff can interfere with that," Redfield told *People* weekly.

And Morgan, known for living modestly, told *Publisher's Weekly,* "I believe I am accountable and steward for all

energy that comes my way, including money." She reportedly has donated thousands of her books to prisons, shel-
ters and other institutions. An appropriate gesture, considering her book uniquely shows how ridiculous a culture can
be when it becomes too attached to material possessions.

"We've worked hard at trying to keep our material lives
the same," Evans said of his success. "There's a lot of challenges that come with money. People want things from you.
But we just want to keep our lives normal."

No, despite how appetizing the view may be from the outside looking in, the biggest reward offered by best-seller
status, say these writers, isn't financial. The real thrill,
they say, is having their words greedily read by so many
people. Some in several foreign languages. Don't misunder-
stand, there are no martyrs here. The big advances, the
cushy author tours with all the trimmings, the great rights
deals and the star treatment isn't being turned down by
anybody. But it's just part of the publishing game, and
these authors are playing that game and playing it well.

But there is more at work here than good ideas, daunt-
less writers and a ready audience. The financial success,
loyal readers and notice from major publishing companies
is proof that the publishing industry is changing, possibly
forever. The term "publishing house," long used to describe
individual book production companies, provides an apt
metaphor. There is a major remodeling job going on in publishing today, and the authors within these pages are its
master carpenters. They are breaking down rules that were
once seen as permanent walls. And they're replacing them
with new rules of their own; opening the doors of musty
rooms and letting in light, ideas and energy.

'Self-published' is no longer a label slapped on books so mediocre they couldn't attract attention from major publishing houses. And small publishing companies, some springing up from the success of a single self-published title, are taking risks on innovative manuscripts from unknown authors that larger companies can't, or won't.

But more importantly, each of these writer's stories can't help but inspire writers who have unpublished manuscripts languishing in a drawer somewhere, that they can do it, too. The large New York publishing houses may be the ones anteing up with the cash to make the big rights deals, secure broad distribution to bookstores and launch slick marketing campaigns, but there wouldn't be a property to bargain for if it weren't for the insight, determination and just plain guts exhibited by small and self publishers. New York no longer dictates what the nation reads, consumers do. People buy what they'd like to read, regardless of who it is published by. And increasingly, they like small and self-published titles.

"The irony of the situation has been noted more than once," writes Jacob Steinberg, Founder of Twayne Publishers, Inc., in *I Never Had a Best-Seller: The Story of a Small Publisher.* "The big firms cannot knowingly undertake publication of the sure losers. Only the small firms with their limited overhead can undertake these books."

Increasingly, these are the companies, and the writers, putting interesting and original books on the shelves of bookstores, libraries and your living room even when there are no huge sales projections, no best-seller promise.

But far from publishing "sure losers," these are also the publishers giving hope to the new talent so eagerly sought after by the Random Houses, the Simon & Schusters, the HarperCollins and the Scribner & Sons of the publishing world.

According to Marilyn Ross, of the Small Publishers Association of North America (SPAN), "Mainstream publishing houses love this trend because they prospect among these books for proven new titles to pick up. This approach saves them editing, typesetting, often cover design time and expense – a real boon in today's downsized companies."

And Suzanne Mantell writes in *Publishers Weekly,* "Self-published successes are nothing new. . . But their availability as a ready-made resource and the profits to be reaped from them have increased their appeal as publishers' lists have grown leaner, authors hungrier, entrepreneurs savvier and technology more accessible. One publisher, Random House, even offers financial rewards to sales reps who keep their ears especially close to the ground." Random House's incentive program reportedly pays a $500 finder's fee for any book published and an additional $1500 if the title makes *The New York Times* best-seller list.

Mantell continues, "Whatever the (sales) numbers, the entrepreneurial spirit and marketing know-how of many self-published authors are a major draw."

And Rick Horgan, former executive editor at HarperCollins and editor of *Mutant Message Down Under,* told *Publishers Weekly,* "More money is being spent on fewer titles, and a lot of people can't get their books placed. This is one reason people are going the self-published route. Another reason is the money to be made. And there's validation."

As a matter of fact, the phenomenon is becoming common enough that it even has more than validation, it has a name – republishing.

But is there a formula? Can you add a pinch of national appeal, a bit of insight, a chunk of just plain great writing and a splash of inspiration and create a best selling book? Even if there were such a formula, conventional publishing wisdom holds that best-sellers can't be created, anyway. Julie Bennett, co-author of *50 Simple Things You Can Do To Save The Earth,* put it this way: "The thing about a best-seller is that nobody can create one," she said. "A lot of people try, but books, once they leave your office, take on a life of their own and they're either going to hit a vein or they're not."

The publishing industry has always held that best-seller lists tabulated by *The New York Times, Publishers Weekly* and others are tamper-proof. Even so, allegations were made in a *Business Week* article (never proven) that Michael Treacy and Fred Wiersema, business management consultants and co-authors of *The Discipline of Market Leaders* (Addison-Wesley, 1995) manipulated their sales, and essentially compromised the integrity of *The New York Times* best-seller list.

The allegations point to the co-authors targeting bookstores that submit sales records to the *Times.* According to the article, they then allegedly arranged for a management firm they're affiliated with (CSC Index) to purchase various quantities of the book from those bookstores. The book did make the *Times* nonfiction list for 15 weeks, with a debut on Feb. 26, 1995.

Such a scheme may not be illegal, but it would certainly

be highly unethical. Both Treacy and Wiersema denied the allegations, and Addison-Wesley publisher David Goehring called them "outrageous and naive" in a letter to *Business Week*. In that letter he contended the book made it onto the *Time's* best-seller list because of, "a 30-city author tour, extensive media coverage, bookstore appearances, corporate seminars and saturation advertising in newspapers, magazines, billboards and radio..." But the controversy can't help but bring to mind suggestion # 47 from *Life's Little Instruction Book* - "Don't waste time learning the 'tricks of the trade.' Instead, learn the trade."

It is interesting that, in his laundry list explaining the book's best-seller status, Goehring made no mention of the quality, timeliness or originality of the book itself. Whether the story is true or not, it certainly underscores the influence wielded by such lists, their power to create celebrities, bank accounts, client lists, careers, respect and even awe. The awe surrounding the lists themselves can't help but be transferred to the authors whose names appear there. According to *USA Today*, best-seller lists have far-reaching effects. Bookstore buyers read them to make sure they've got the books people are buying. Librarians use them to make sure they've got the books people are borrowing. Corporate vendors read them to make sure they're keeping up with the market. And consumers read it for advice on what book to buy next.

But it appears that various combinations of the three characteristics not mentioned by Goehring – quality, timeliness, originality – is exactly what propelled the books profiled here onto best-seller lists, without any bells or whistles. Most had no marketing or advertising budgets until after they had been through several printings, or the author had sold the rights to a large publishing company. No 30-city author tours or four-color lighted billboards for these books. No radio talk shows, no Oprah appearances, no inside cover ads in *The New York Times Book Review*. Not in their early stages, anyway .

The cliché of struggling authors selling copies of their precious books out of the trunks of their cars is as familiar in publishing circles as the words, "Once upon a time..." But the clichés really happened! Redfield actually did pack the trunk of his car with books, and sold them door-to-bookstore door. So did John Jabna, co-author of *50 Simple Things You Can Do To Save The Earth,* and Greg Godek, author of *1,001 Ways To Be Romantic*.

And indeed the stories have already become industry fairy tales. And the stuff of dreams for not just authors, but editors, too. Every new editor and even a few seasoned ones are on the lookout for the next Marlo Morgan, the next James Redfield, the next Richard Paul Evans. Maybe that could be you!

inside the BEST SELLERS

1

$\mathcal{T}$he $\mathcal{C}$hristmas $\mathcal{B}$ox

by Richard Paul Evans

"The message concerns love, of course, and the strings Evans pulls to vivify it should squeezes sobs from even the stoniest of hearts."

– Publishers Weekly

The Christmas Box just isn't big enough. Now we're not talking about the book of the same name. That, on the contrary, has proven itself in innumerable news accounts to be plenty big. But rather, we're talking about the actual box itself. In the book, author Richard Paul Evans gives the dimensions of the "ornate wooden box of burled walnut" as "about ten inches wide, fourteen inches long, and a half foot deep." And that, according to Citibank, is nowhere near big enough to hold the $4.2 million Simon & Schuster reportedly paid for the rights to the hardcover and audio versions of the book and its prequel, *Timepiece*.

Like most of the books profiled, *The Christmas Box* had meager beginnings prior to scoring the multi-book, multi-million dollar publishing deal. Evans, a 34-year-old Mormon advertising executive from Salt Lake City, originally wrote the novella in 1992 as an expression of fatherly love for his two daughters, Jenna, then six, and Allyson, then four.

"Even though I told them all the time that I loved them, I didn't think they could ever really understand the depth of those feelings until they had raised their own children, and by that time our relationship would have already changed," said Evans. "I wanted to express my love to my girls in a way that would be timeless."

And timeless is exactly what Simon & Schuster is hoping the title will turn out to be. Although certainly bound by seasonal sales, the theme of the novella isn't year specific, making it a possible annual October, November and December best-seller for years to come. The publisher is counting on people who either bought it themselves or got it as a gift last Christmas to give it as a gift this Christmas, and next Christmas, too. A good bet, considering its sales history.

"Where we thought we'd sell 3,000 books over the 1993 Christmas season, we sold 3,000 a day," Evans said. "I didn't expect anything at first. When it became the number one book in every bookstore we sold it to, then I knew that if we handled it right, it would become the number one book in the country."

The next holiday season, after Simon & Schuster controlled the rights, the hardcover version first appeared on *Publishers Weekly's* best-seller List on November 6, 1995, at number 14, and by December 11 was firmly in the coveted number one spot. It's available in at least 30 countries and has been translated into 13 languages.

Evans reportedly wrote the 87-page Christian-based tale in six weeks, and credits a 4 a.m. bolt of divine intervention with revealing the story to him at while he was sitting at his kitchen table.

"It really was a miracle because the story started to write itself," Evans said. "It would just flood into my mind in torrents of inspiration. It would wake me up in the middle of the night. Once I pulled off the freeway and wrote part of a chapter. I wrote on the backs of envelopes and bills and any scraps of paper I could find in the car. That story has probably been reported a thousand times, but it's true."

The Christmas Box story begins with the narrator, Richard, setting out to tell the tale of the Christmas Box (possibly made by St. Nick from the trunk of the very first Christmas tree) before it is forgotten, lost forever to future generations.

"Whatever the reason, I find that with each passing Christmas the story of the Christmas Box is told less and needed more," begins the story. "So I record it now for all future generations to accept or dismiss as seems them good. As for me, I believe. And it is, after all, my story."

Richard and his family (bearing the same names as the author's family) move in with a kind but mysteriously sad widow, Mary, and agree to help with the chores at her Victorian mansion in exchange for room and board.

Evans made 20 photocopies to share with family and friends, and within three weeks those tattered, worn copies had been read by 160 people to the rave reviews every

Richard Paul Evans

"The Christmas Box *is still probably the biggest book I'll ever write, but that's not disappointing. Say one of your children grows up to be President of the United States. That doesn't mean you won't be proud of your other children for their accomplishments.*"

literary wanna-be dreams of. And so spurred on by words of encouragement from that widening circle of family and friends, the former advertising executive decided to send the manuscript to a few regional publishers. When it was rejected, he sent it to other publishing houses which also reportedly rejected it for the same reasons the smaller companies did; too short, too seasonal.

The new industry adage, 'If you can't get a book done right (or at all), do it yourself,' was not lost on Evans. Taking rejection in stride, he spent $5,000 to have 8,000 copies of a $4.95 paperback version of the book printed and distributed to Utah bookstores. When those sold, he spent $13,000 to have another 19,000 copies printed.

"I had the money because I had just completed an advertising contract," he said.

Within weeks it was the most sought-after book in the state and by the end of 1994, 250,000 copies of the self-published title were distributed nationally. Obviously, Evans was quite skilled in putting his advertising and marketing expertise to use in the publishing world.

"The selling was done from bookstore to bookstore," he said. "But had I not had the advertising experience, I don't know if we could have done it."

It wasn't until this sentimental holiday tale hit the paperback best-seller list that it caught the attention of Simon & Schuster rookie editor Laurie Chittenden. She was reading an article about Evans in *People* weekly, and decided to investigate a rights deal.

"Self-published books are really a good route for an assistant editor to go," she told *Publishers Weekly*. "It's hard to get agents to send manuscripts."

So this young editor who had only been in the publishing business for a year, and at Simon & Schuster for a month, got in on one of the biggest rags-to-riches publishing stories of the year.

Evans has been busy since all heck (this is a Christian story, remember?) broke loose. He wrote *Timepiece* and it has since been released to mixed reviews. He went on a 31-city author tour courtesy of Simon & Schuster. His wife, Keri, gave birth to a third daughter, Abigail Hope, and the couple may adopt a fourth child. *The Christmas Box* was also made into a television movie starring Maureen O'Hara as Mary and Richard Thomas as Richard. Thomas also narrates the audio book version of the title.

Evans' second book, *Timepiece,* became an instant bestseller, probably much to the company's relief.

"Every time I would start to write (*Timepiece*), it would stop, almost like I was writing the wrong story," he said. "Then one day I was out for a walk, and I was thinking about all of the research I had done on scarlet fever, and it occurred to me, (the character) didn't die of scarlet fever, she died in a fire. I ran home and I wrote out the head of every chapter. I told my wife, I called my agent, I called my editor. My editor was very relieved. She was very nervous about the project. They had paid a lot of money, but hadn't ever seen me write."

And though the process is hard work, Evans said he pictures himself as a life-long writer, so his fans can look forward to more of his books in the future. He is currently working on the third book in the family story, yet to be titled.

"My books are getting better," he said. *"The Christmas*

Box is still probably the biggest book I'll ever write, but that's not disappointing. Say one of your children grows up to be President of the United States. That doesn't mean you won't be proud of your other children for their accomplishments."

Writing, author tours, speaking engagements and attending writer's conferences takes Evans away from his family frequently, and has caused a bit of a predicament for the writer. In *The Christmas Box,* the main character, Richard, is repeatedly chastised for the lack of time he spends with his family, and especially with his young daughter. Evans said he has to be very careful he doesn't make it a case of life imitating art.

"It's a horrible paradox," he said. "It's difficult. When I was getting ready to leave on my author tour, Jenna was crying. I was going to be gone for three weeks. But the reality of it is, I spend more time with my family than most dads. And when I'm home, I'm really home. Time wise, we're better off when I was in advertising."

Part of that time away is spent at writers conferences, advising others on self-publishing, and how to be successful at it. He frequently uses this analogy:

"Say you dress your kid in ugly clothes and send them to school on the first day. What happens? Everyone makes fun of them and no one will play with them. Ninety-nine percent of the time, you can tell a self-published title by looking at it. That is completely fatal. Bookstores don't want to carry it and people don't want to buy it. Remember, you're competing with Warner Books and Simon & Schuster. It handicaps your book. Go for simplicity and beauty and make it look like something Hyperion put out. Go to a bookstore, and copy the fonts they're using."

And, he said *The Christmas Box* was successful in spite of being self-published, not because of it.

"If you look at the odds, I had a better chance of winning the Idaho lottery than writing a best-seller."

But for those who persevere, Evans advises them to grow regionally, and, "be very careful. Don't quit your job and put up your house. I did, but only after three years of it being the best-selling book in every bookstore we got it in."

When you close the back cover of *The Christmas Box,* and finish reading it, Evans said he hopes you take away whatever emotional or spiritual message your life was missing when you opened it and started reading.

"I hope it gives them what they need most. What I mean by that is that if people feel lonely, they have companionship. If they're missing someone, they feel comforted. If they are just in a hurry and don't appreciate Christmas, I hope it gives them perspective."

Many readers have been able to do that, if the attention the angel statue has gotten is any indication. At the end of the story, the widow Mary is found by Richard in a cemetery, weeping over her long-dead child. A note says that for comfort, readers can send notes and flowers to the statue, seeking their own salvation.

"They still get 15 to 20 calls every day," Evans said, of the cemetery office. "Tour buses go there. The angel is covered by flowers every day. I'll drive up there just to meditate, and there will always already be someone there. We finally took maps of how to get to the angel because so many people were asking for directions."

"No one can give faith unless he has faith. It is the persuaded who persuade."

– Joseph Joubert

*I*n the rain forests of Peru, an ancient manuscript has been discovered.
Within its pages are 9 key insights into life itself – insights each human being
is predicted to grasp sequentially, one insight then another, as we move toward
a completely spiritual culture on Earth.

THE
CELESTINE
PROPHECY
AN ADVENTURE

James Redfield

"A fabulous book about experiencing life–I couldn't put it down."
–Elisabeth Kübler-Ross, M.D.

2

THE
CELESTINE
PROPHECY
AN ADVENTURE
by James Redfield

*"A fabulous book about experiencing life –
I couldn't put it down."*

– Elisabeth Kubler-Ross, M.D.

The claims on the dark green book jacket are certainly ambitious. "YOU HAVE NEVER READ A BOOK LIKE THIS BEFORE," the gold type proclaims. *"THE CELESTINE PROPHECY* CONTAINS SECRETS THAT ARE CURRENTLY CHANGING OUR WORLD," and "A BOOK THAT COMES ALONG ONCE IN A LIFE-TIME TO CHANGE LIVES FOREVER." Now those are some pretty bold promises. But the real story here is that, surprisingly enough, for many readers, the book delivers.

Despite one bad review after another, *The Celestine Prophecy* has made good on enough of those blatantly ambitious promises to sell 5.5 million books. One hundred and fifty thousand of those were self-published copies of the title, sold to individuals and bookstores by author James Redfield, before he signed over the hardcover rights to Warner Books for a reported $800,000 in December, 1993. The book's widely admitted faults: it's not particularly well written and is filled with logical inconsistency and historical errors. *The Minneapolis Star Tribune* called it, "New Age pop psychology in the form of a bad novel. . . to categorize this as literature makes no more sense than calling a connect-the-dots painting a work of art." Ouch! And from *The National Review,* ". . .a tenth-rate melodrama joining Gnostic hubris with flower-child theology."

Everyone has an opinion, but apparently former flower children, now 30-some years older and preoccupied with their spiritual destinies, are buying books. And *The Celestine Prophecy's* unique way of packaging sacred theories into an adventure novel without even a hint of preachyness, appeals to the New Age market, as well as the huge numbers of readers who categorize themselves as spiritual, but not religious.

The "Nine Insights" which form the core of the novel and move the plot along at a good clip, could not have been written by someone who did not come of age during the 1960's. Redfield, 47, grew up outside Birmingham, Ala., in a Methodist family, the son of an artist father and homemaker mother. He majored in psychology at Auburn University, in Auburn, Ala., earning a master's degree in counseling and putting it to use with troubled teenagers.

During this time he was also continually formulating his own spiritual ideas, mostly about the role of nature in human spiritual growth. Those ideas eventually led to the book, but it was not solely based on fantasy.

In a radical departure from the day-to-day lives of most of us; work, responsibility, routine, Redfield left the Heart of Dixie and traveled to the Peruvian Andes in the mid 1970s. While there he heard about a missing ancient document, rumored to reveal the meaning of life. Did he find it? Well, it was on that trip that Redfield says the seeds of the novel were planted, but only came into flower in 1989 when he quit his job as a children's therapist to write full-time.

While writing the book he became a regular fixture at a Birmingham Waffle House restaurant. It was a good place to write, he says, because it kept him focused on his prospective audience: everyday people with everyday problems and spiritual needs. "That helped give me a sense of a generic audience, to keep the story simple," he told *People* weekly. Maybe all you waffle eaters out there are more spiritual than you think.

The protagonist of *Prophecy* is a disenchanted baby-boomer, a burned-out counselor of troubled teenagers, unable to form lasting relationships and searching for a way to inject his life with meaning. This is more than a bit autobiographical, as Redfield was that counselor, drained by 15 years of emotional outlay, and went through a divorce, after a brief first marriage failed in the late 1970s. Sounds also like your run-of-the mill middle-class drone suffering an all-too-cliched mid-life crisis, but there are some profound messages here, too. For example, ". . . love is not an intellectual concept or a moral imperative or

James Redfield

"The old Newtonian idea is that everything happens by chance, that one can make good decisions and be prepared, but that every event has its own line of causation independent of our attitude. After the recent discoveries of modern physics, we may legitimately ask if the universe is more dynamic than that."

anything else. It is a background emotion that exists when one is connected to the energy available in the universe, which, of course, is the energy of God," says book character Father Sanchez, a wise Peruvian priest.

And, "The old Newtonian idea is that everything happens by chance, that one can make good decisions and be prepared, but that every event has its own line of causation independent of our attitude. After the recent discoveries of modern physics, we may legitimately ask if the universe is more dynamic than that," states a scientific researcher.

The main character embarks on a dangerous trek through the Peruvian Andes, in search of a manuscript dating to 600 BC, that promises to hold nine insights which will propel humans to a totally spiritual culture on earth. These insights, a mix of Carl Jung's synchronicity theory, Universalism, quantum physics, Eastern mysticism and select parts of the Ten Commandments, center around the idea of a spiritual science.

"Are three decades of interest in modern physics, ecology, mystical religion and interpersonal psychology finally synthesizing into a new spiritual common sense?" inquires the book's jacket text. "Are we beginning to live this new common sense?"

Maybe it was this "spiritual common sense" that supported Redfield throughout the process of writing and selling his novel. The author himself is convinced that some higher power was present. "I'm reluctant to say I was chosen," Redfield said. "But I certainly was driven."

With a completed manuscript and a string of rejection letters in hand, the author emptied his savings account, and in December 1992 spent $13,000 to have 3,000 copies printed. He then established Satori Publishing, named for a Japanese Buddhist term loosely translated as "instant enlightenment and spiritual awakening."

Then he and new bride Salle Merrill, a former massage therapist, packed them in the trunk of his Honda Accord, went on an extended road trip, and sold them to New Age bookstores across the South.

At a recent appearance at The New Age Metaphysical Exposition in Denver, Colo., Redfield attributed his success to something that could not happen in the superstore bookstores, but only in independent bookstores. He developed personal relationships with the people he met when dropping off his book, they in turn recommended it to their customers, much as local librarians recommended books to their regular readers. One good turn synchronistically led to another, and Redfield made several trips back to the printer, ultimately selling an unheard of 150,000 self-published copies of the book. That was enough to attract the attention of some major New York publishers, a bidding war ensued, with Warner Books coming out on top.

There are currently five movie companies bidding on the film rights to the book, Redfield receives hundreds of fan letters every week and the sequel, *The Tenth Insight,* released by Warner Books in April 1996, landed at the #2 spot on *Publishers Weekly's* fiction best-seller list after being on sale for less than a week. It had a first printing of one million copies and the publisher sent Redfield on an eight city tour – and you can bet it wasn't in a beat up Honda.

In an audio review of Redfield's second book, a *Publishers Weekly* reviewer wrote, "At the rate Redfield's following is growing, he may just end up like the late science fiction writer L. Ron Hubbard and spawn his own quasi-religion."

Aside from his success as an author, Redfield has also developed the Nine Insights from *The Celestine Prophecy* into a side business. There is a $29.95 newsletter, *The Celestine Journal,* available at his web site, The Celestine Network (the World Wide Web address is http://pathfinder.com/@VWS5KAQAORik*lfm/twep/Features/Celestine/) and a personalized $49.95 audio tape based on an individual's sun and moon signs.

There are also hundreds of Celestine study groups that popped up all across the country, continuing to meet and discuss *The Tenth Insight.* Redfield and his wife also occasionally run workshops themselves on the books. There is a limited edition of *The Tenth Insight* available for $50, with royalties being donated to inner city reading projects and a campaign to protect old growth forests. He is also working with author Michael Murphy (*Future of the Body*) on a book and compact disc delving into the past 30 years of spiritual history.

But despite having plenty of spin-off products to sell, Redfield has generally stayed away from the free publicity offered by the talk show circuit, and opted for the more tranquil surroundings at his Florida beach house, or his newly built home in Stoney Butte, Alabama.

There he finds peace to work on his yet-to-be-announced (but anxiously awaited) next project, and to crank out a screenplay for the movie version of the book(s). And maybe even use a little of that coveted peace and quiet to savor his success. There is certainly no sin in using one's talent to make other people's lives a little more introspective, a little more uplifted, even if outrageous success is part of the bargain.

"Bringing out the best in others rather than having power over them introduces a concept that makes inherent sense for spiritual growth as an attainable reality," wrote book reviewer and social worker Ruth L. Rosen, in *Addiction Letter*.

Ah, the life of a successful, self-published author. Adventure, riches, happiness and your own and others' spiritual enlightenment in the process. What better way to make a living is there than that?

"Money and fame don't automatically make people happy. It has to come from within. Chicken Soup For The Soul will put a million smiles in your heart."

Robin Leach, host,
Lifestyles Of The Rich And Famous

Chicken Soup for the Soul™

101 Stories To Open The Heart And Rekindle The Spirit

With Outstanding Stories By:
Dan Millman
Robert Fulghum
Gloria Steinem
Tony Robbins
Art Buchwald
Les Brown
And Many,
Many More

WRITTEN & COMPILED BY

Jack Canfield
Mark Victor Hansen

3

Chicken Soup
for the Soul

by Jack Canfield and Mark Victor Hansen

"Those un-Gumped grumps among us might say Chicken Soup for the Soul *could be subtitled* Oatmeal for the Brain. *Each story can easily be read in one trip to the bathroom, and you could sop up the entire chapter on 'Learning to Love Yourself' while waiting in the dentist's office.* The Bridges of Madison County *is* Anna Karenina *by comparison."*

– *The Los Angeles Times*

Bosnia. Drive-by shootings. Corporate downsizing. Alzheimer's disease. Homeless kids. What the world needs is a big, steaming bowl of homemade spiritual chicken soup. Meet master word chefs, Jack Canfield and Mark Victor Hansen, authors of *Chicken Soup for the Soul*. The special of the day? Hotcakes. As in – selling like.

Who can resist stories like the following:

The Gift

"Bennet Cerf relates this touching story about a bus that was bumping along a back road in the South.

In one seat a wispy old man sat holding a bunch of fresh flowers. Across the aisle was a young girl whose eyes came back again and again to the man's flowers. The time came for the old man to get off. Impulsively he thrust the flowers into the girl's lap. 'I can see you love the flowers,' he explained, 'and I think my wife would like for you to have them. I'll tell her I gave them to you.' The girl accepted the flowers, then watched the old man get off the bus and walk through the gate of a small cemetery."

Published in June of 1993 by Health Communications, Inc. of Deerfield Beach, Fla., the anthology of inspirational anecdotes has been on *The New York Times* bestseller list since September 1994 (consecutively for over 90 weeks) and has sold over 11 million copies. In 1995, the book won the American Booksellers Association (ABA) 'Book of the Year' award (ABBY award). The coveted award is given annually by the ABA to the book that booksellers most enjoyed personally recommending to their customers. The book has since been translated into 21 languages and been featured in every major magazine from *People* weekly to *Forbes* to *Library Journal.* Not bad for a manuscript that was turned down by 30 publishers for being, "too nicey-nice."

"I think a lot of people just need to be uplifted," Canfield said. "We knew in our hearts it would do well, but we really had no idea we'd get this kind of incredible response. We tapped into something universal in people without really even knowing it."

Best buddies for 16 years, fathers, husbands and motivational speakers, the pair used stories from their lectures and workshops as the impetus for the book, adding vignettes by such well-known personalities as Robert Fulghum, Gloria Steinem, Tony Robbins and Art Buchwald. The 101 stories are grouped into sections with names like, "Live Your Dream," "On Love," and "Overcoming Obstacles." Though the pair credits the book's success to its easy-to-read format and accessible language, Health Communications President Peter Vegso thinks differently.

"They were a publisher's dream," Vegso told *The Los Angeles Times.* "Their energy and enthusiasm didn't end when the book was published. They worked hard on marketing and promoting it everywhere they went."

Canfield and Hansen both said they're proud of the fact that they literally never turned down an interview. Whether it was a writer's support group newsletter or *The New York Times,* they were talking. Their goal, inspired by advice from M. Scott Peck (author of *The Road Less Traveled*) was to average one media interview per day,

Jack Canfield

"I think a lot of people just need to be uplifted," Canfield
said. *"We knew in our hearts it would do well, but we really
had no idea we'd get this kind of incredible response. We
tapped into something universal in people without really
even knowing it."*

every year. On many occasions they've put that goal to shame by doing phone interviews for radio shows and newspapers and appearing on television talk shows all in the same day.

Canfield once estimated that in a single 24-hour period, the pair reached 12 million listeners by giving satellite radio interviews on a grueling 20-minute revolving schedule. Their dogged pursuit of publicity for their book earned them *Radio-TV Interview Report's* Distinguished Author Award. The trade magazine is poured over by 4,000 television and radio producers looking for authors, experts and celebrities to be guests on their shows.

"I was really so struck by their willingness to do any interview, any time," said Stephen Hall of *Radio-TV Interview Report*. "So many authors make the mistake of having an attitude that they'll only do the top radio or the top TV. Or, they make the mistake of only promoting their book the first three months after it comes out. One of the reasons that Jack and Mark have been so successful is that they formed the habit of promoting themselves. One of the advantages of having that attitude is that you never know which interview is going to be the one that sells. You never know who is listening. By forming the habit, it ultimately snowballs into great publishing success."

The pair learned early on exactly how much of a book's success depends upon great public relations and marketing. Soon after the book was published they interviewed several best-selling authors including the afore mentioned M. Scott Peck, but also Barbara De Angelis, Harvey MacKay, Wayne Dyer and Betty Eadie, and asked them what it took to be successful.

Mark Victor Hansen

"I can keep up the enthusiasm because I genuinely am more excited about it," he said. "We have bigger opportunities to reach people. Stories are living beings. You share them, and the images within go to work."

"The bottom line is that 90 percent of what it takes to succeed is publicity, marketing and promoting," said Hansen. "The biggest mistake most authors make is that they do a 20-day tour and think they've finished promoting their book. The first year, we were doing a minimum of one interview a day, seven days a week. We were willing to do radio interviews at three in the morning in Montana or Alabama. A great book no one knows about is absolutely useless."

Thanks to their strategy, now everyone knows about *Chicken Soup for the Soul*. If there are a few stragglers left that haven't heard, Canfield and Hansen have them in their sights. Thus far the title has been featured on *CBS Eye to Eye*, in *People* weekly magazine, *The Los Angeles Times*, *The New York Times*, *USA Today*, *Entrepreneur*, *Forbes*, *Good Housekeeping*, *Library Journal* and hundreds of other publications and television and radio shows. And they continue to give interviews, make public appearances and show up at book-signings. Fully three years after the book was published, Canfield told Stephen Hall, "We're still doing radio and TV like mad dogs."

While the pair certainly are the exposure experts, it's not just empty promotion, but work inspired by their genuine commitment to the book's central message: hope for humanity. That may sound a bit hokey, or "nicey-nice," but when you talk with these guys, you can tell they mean it. Hansen said that he is more excited about the book today than when it was first published.

"I can keep up the enthusiasm because I genuinely am more excited about it," he said. "We have bigger opportunities to reach people. Stories are living beings. You share them, and the images within go to work."

And they've even put some of their money where their mouth is. They donated the $5,000 ABBY award prize money to the Soup Kitchens for the Soul Project, an organization dedicated to helping people in prisons, inner city schools and other programs for at-risk adults and teenagers and people in crisis.

"Because of the tremendous success surrounding *Chicken Soup for the Soul,* we want to share some of our good fortune with those in need," Canfield said. "We get hundreds of letters every day from people telling us that the book has helped someone get through a very hard time in their life."

Another donation is being made by the authors and Health Communications, Inc. to the American Red Cross. Part of the proceeds from *A 3rd Serving of Chicken Soup for the Soul* (.50 cents per book sold) are being donated to the organization's Soup For Life program to fund its vital lifesaving services. And they are just getting involved with a nation-wide literacy project.

In their roles as motivational speakers, the authors teach attendees how to visualize success. Practicing what they preach, they found a unique way to use the mental tool themselves, after the book was published.

"Mark and I visualized *Chicken Soup for the Soul* being number one on *The New York Times* best-seller list for almost a year," said Canfield. "Can you believe that we actually cut the list out of the paper, whited out the number one book and wrote in our book? It's framed and hanging in both of our offices."

Other advice from the book-selling gurus: set up a 1-800

number to fill book orders, always give your radio or TV audience an incentive to order today, and be prepared for your interviews.

Since the success of *Chicken Soup for the Soul,* there has been some remarkable spin-off successes. Health Communications released *A 2nd Helping of Chicken Soup for the Soul* in April 1995, *A 3rd Serving of Chicken Soup for the Soul* in April 1996, *Chicken Soup for the Soul Cookbook* in October 1995, *Chicken Soup for the Surviving Soul* also in May 1996, and this past fall released *Chicken Soup for the Woman's Soul, Chicken Soup for the Soul at Work,* a *Cup of Chicken Soup for the Soul* and *Condensed Chicken Soup for the Soul.*

All of the spin-off titles use the story as a universal metaphor to communicate across gender, cultural, age and language barriers.

"After reading the reports of how our first book powerfully touched so many lives, we are now more convinced than ever that stories are one of the most potent ways to transform our lives," reads the introduction to *A 3rd Serving.* "They speak directly to the subconscious mind. They lay down blueprints for living. They awaken us from our habitual day-to-day lives, invite us to dream, and inspire us to do more and be more than we might have originally thought possible."

Plans are in the works for a television show on ABC based on the *Chicken Soup* books, and the authors have begun offering workshops for writers seeking to turn their words into a speaking/publishing career. And the next project? Well, right now, Hansen said he's just trying to come up with an end to the following story.

"We have an herb garden at my house and 28 animals, and kids and the works. My daughter likes butterflies, and she puts all the caterpillars on a certain plant to keep them safe from the birds, and make more butterflies. Well, one day there was a butterfly just emerging from the cocoon, and it's wings were so wet and fragile, that one of them tore right off. She was so sad, and kept asking 'Daddy can I keep him, Daddy can I keep him.' And I told her he couldn't possibly live, but she kept asking, and so of course I said yes. Well for three nights she slept with that damaged little butterfly on her chest, and never rolled over in the night and smashed it. It was always right there when she woke up. Finally on the third day, it died. We had a proper burial and ceremony. I was so touched by my daughter's kindness."

The ending hasn't come to him yet, but it will.

"Every author has great stories," Hansen said. "Every author has flaming hoops and and death-defying acts. We're just getting started."

"Everything comes to him
who hustles while he waits."

– Thomas A. Edison

The National #1 Bestseller!
50
SIMPLE
THINGS
YOU
CAN DO TO
SAVE THE
EARTH
THE EARTH•WORKS GROUP

4

50 Simple Things You Can Do To Save The Earth

by The Earth Works Group

Julienne Bennett's favorite "thing" is snipping six-pack rings.

"I rarely buy soft drinks but when I do I can't throw the plastic rings away without cutting them in half first," she said. "That is the heart of the book – simple actions that can have a profound effect on our planet."

Bennett is the co-publisher, with John Javna, of *50 Simple Things You Can Do To Save The Earth* by The Earth Works Group (Earth Works Press, 1989). The slim volume offers 50 practical ways to improve the environment by making small changes in daily actions. The $4.95 paperback spent seven months on *The New York Times* best-seller list, was featured on nation-wide television and

Julienne Bennett

"I believe nobody can 'create' a bestseller. A lot of people try. Every year hundreds of authors write interesting, intelligent texts, which their publishers edit, design, and print with great care and attention to detail. But once a book leaves the warehouse it takes on a life of its own."

radio shows and was written about in major magazines and newspapers including *Time, Newsweek* and *The Wall Street Journal*. Ultimately it sold over 4.5 million copies and earned a place in American popular culture.

Like every one of the 60,000 books published annually, *50 Simple Things You Can Do To Save The Earth* started with an idea. Julienne, then Vice-president and Director of Marketing at Emeryville, California-based Publishers Group West, and John, an experienced author and book packager, wanted to collaborate on a book. The upcoming twentieth anniversary of Earth Day sparked the project. Together, they created the concept for the book. John researched and managed the writing and editorial work, Julienne did the sales and marketing. In October of 1989, John drained his savings account to pay for the first 25,000 copies. They sold immediately and the pair went back to the printer once more before Christmas that same year, ordering 15,000 additional copies.

After Christmas, sales continued to escalate and the entrepreneurs realized they were completely unprepared for their success. For starters, they didn't even have a working office. They were faced with having to create inventory, accounts payable and receivable systems, open checking accounts, hire and train a staff and buy computers and office equipment almost overnight.

"Those were interesting times," recalls Bennett. "We worked almost every night until three or four in the morning. In the midst of all the excitement and turmoil John looked at me one day and said, 'You know, it's like trying to change drivers when you're going 100 miles per hour.' "

In January 1990 the book appeared on *The New York Times* best-sellers list, and by March, as the 20th anniversary of Earth Day approached, it was selling at a phenomenal rate.

"We could barely keep up with the demand," Bennett recalled. "The print runs got bigger and bigger but we were always out of stock. It's one thing to order 400,000 books and know they have all been sold. It's another thing to see that many books in one place. It can only be described as a great wall of books. I remember walking by pallet after pallet of books in our warehouse – it seemed as though they went on forever. I'll never forget it – 400,000 books are a lot of books."

Today, Javna, who has since published many best-selling books, is revising *50 Simple Things You Can Do To Save The Earth* for the millennium. Bennett left Publishers Group West to become a partner at Conari Press where she came up with the original idea for several other successful books including *Random Acts of Kindness* and *The Woman's Book of Courage*. Today she is a partner in Circulus Publishing Group, Inc., and publisher of Berkeley, California-based Wildcat Canyon Press. Her partners at Circulus describe her ability to conceive, package and market a book as magical, the result of a highly-developed intuitive sense of what people are feeling and want to read about. Their most recent success is *Girlfriends* by Tamara Traeder and Carmen Renee Berry (1995) which has over 160,000 copies in print. But she remains nothing if not pragmatic about this phenomenon called a best-seller.

"I believe nobody can 'create' a best-seller," she said.

"A lot of people try. Every year hundreds of authors write interesting, intelligent texts, which their publishers edit, design, and print with great care, and attention to detail. But once a book leaves the warehouse it takes on a life of its own. It's either going to hit a nerve or not. We were lucky, *50 Simple Things* hit a nerve. And it was really fun."

A numbered listing
creative, unusual & wonderful
ideas, gifts & gestures

1·0·0·1

Ways To Be

ROMANTIC

◆

Gregory J.P. Godek

For
Men and Women
✦
Young and Old
✦
Singles and Marrieds

*"Greg Godek should
be nominated for the
Nobel Peace Prize for
teaching 1001 Ways
to be Romantic"*

~ Boston Magazine

5

1001 Ways to be Romantic

by Greg Godek

If romance had a deed, Greg Godek's name would be on it. Author of *1001 Ways to be Romantic,* president of Casablanca Press, Inc. and self-titled perpetual newlywed, Godek confesses he was romantic long before it became an avocation, then preoccupation, and finally, his occupation.

This 40-year-old, happily married, publishing Romeo is in the midst of a torrid love affair, but don't bother tattling to his wife, she already knows and doesn't even mind. As a matter of fact, she encourages the relationship. The object of his affection is a character most writers don't find romantic, sexy, or even remotely attractive: Marketing. But Godek showers his paramour with big cash outlays, daily attention and every bit of creativity he's got.

"I market all the time," Godek said. "If I'm not doing something, I'm thinking about it. I believe that a publisher's job is marketing. A publisher's job is not producing books. Production and distribution are the easiest things in the world. Now selling books? That takes some work. I've spent hundreds of thousands of dollars in marketing. It requires everything you've got. You need to spend all of your time and more than all of your money on it."

Godek's innovative marketing strategies have enabled him to sell one million copies of his company's flagship book, and this is how he did it:

*He gave away 6,000 copies of the book (his cost: $1 each) to reporters, radio producers, television talk show hosts, well-wishers and others in 1995.

*He spent $20,000 to outfit his exhibit at the 1995 American Booksellers Association show in Chicago.

*He spent $9,000 on a video press release mailed to television stations all across the country just days before Valentine's Day in 1996.

*He spent $25,000 on a three-week, 21-city tour before Valentine's Day in 1996, conducting book-signings, radio interviews and television interviews in each city.

*He spent $6 each on a press kit mailed to hundreds of media personnel across the country.

*He spends $10,000 on photography and $50,000 with his public relations firm (Cone Communications, Boston, Mass.) every year.

*He spent $70,000 on a recreational vehicle, $3,000 for an exterior design of a couple locked in an embrace, and another $12,000 to install the design on the outside of the RV.

Yes, Greg owns romance all right; he's bought and paid for it. And, owning a niche in publishing can be a very powerful, and lucrative, purchase. For example, who owns sex? Dr. Ruth. Computer software? Bill Gates. Cookies? Mrs. Fields. And Godek wants his name to be as recognizable, and his bank account as big, as those entrepreneurs.

"It's a huge advantage, but they're hard to find," Godek said, of niche publishing ownership. "Frankly, I was lucky. Romance? Before me there was a blank."

A blank spot big enough to drive an RV through. And that is exactly what Godek is doing. He and his wife, Tracy, began a two-year, cross-country author tour in February 1996, aiming to sell books to America's romantically challenged. The couple will visit 200 bookstores spread over all 50 states before they're through, and attract more than just a little attention. When a 36-foot, gleaming white RV sporting a 12-foot-tall mural of a couple making out rolls into town, people tend to notice.

"The thing is so amazing looking that frankly, attracting the media is not too difficult," he said. "They stop us before we even have a chance to pitch to them." And when they come running with notepads open, pens poised, cameras on and tapes rolling, he's ready. His press kit includes easily quoted nuggets including ways to be romantic ("Test drive a Porsche together." #695), cute love trivia ("What is the significance of green M&Ms? They're aphrodisiacs."), a self test to determine your RBI (romance brilliance index) and of course, books for sale. Besides *1001 Ways to be Romantic*, Casablanca has also published *The Portable Romantic*, *Lover's Bedside Companion, Loving: A Journal* and *How to Buy a Diamond*, by top diamond-cutter, Fred Cuellar.

Greg Godek

"Time, money and creativity are the only things you have to work with in life, love and even selling books," according to Godek. "Creativity is the only one of the three that is unlimited. This puts small press publishers head and shoulders above the big publishers."

Becoming a publisher was not what Godek intended when, in 1990, he quit his job in freelance public relations to write a book. In two months he turned the notes of a male-only adult education class he was teaching entitled, "How to be Romantic," into a manuscript.

"I didn't start out saying, 'I want to be a publisher,'" he said. "Anybody with a brain knows you can't make a living on a book. I started out with a passion for romance and went straight to self-publishing. Was I going to be begging anybody to publish my book? You must be kidding."

Godek criticized large publishers for having misleading practices in their dealings with first-time authors, saying they "market bestsellers, not books." Most first-time authors are naive about how much effort and expense a large publisher is willing to expend to sell their books, he said, and those people would be better off either self-publishing their manuscript, or submitting it to a small press publisher. Small publishers are open to innovative manuscripts and marketing plans, and are honest about what they will invest in a project, according to Godek.

"Time, money and creativity are the only things you have to work with in life, love and even selling books," according to Godek. "Creativity is the only one of the three that is unlimited. This puts small press publishers head and shoulders above the big publishers. Big publishers have huge staffs, complicated politics and therefore organizational resistance to new ideas."

Godek's personal and professional lives have become so intertwined they seem virtually indistinguishable from each other. And much of his advice on how to be romantic, can be applied to selling books, too. "Way to be Romantic"

#1976: "Add these ingredients, in any combination or measure, to your next romantic gift or gesture: anticipation, intrigue and surprise. Mix well, don't do it half-baked, and serve with a flourish!"

"Love doesn't make the world go 'round. Love is what makes the ride worthwhile."

– Franklin P. Jones

Life's Little Instruction Book

511 suggestions, observations, and reminders
on how to live a happy and rewarding life

6

Life's Little Instruction Book

511 suggestions, observations, and reminders on
how to live a happy and rewarding life

by H. Jackson Brown

"Yeah, it sounds corny, but what the heck.
Some of us find comfort in corn – be it
popped, fermented or dished up in a cutesy
little red-and-green plaid book."

– Susan Watson, Detroit Free Press

"Th
his book began as a gift to my son, Adam. As he
packed his stereo, typewriter, blue blazer, and
other necessities for his new life as a college
freshman, I retreated to the family room to jot down a few
observations and words of counsel I thought he might find
useful.

"I read years ago that it was not the responsibility of

H. Jackson Brown

"Suggestion #123 Learn to listen. Opportunity sometimes knocks very softly."

parents to pave the road for their children, but to provide a road map. That's how I hoped he would use these mind and heart reflections.

"I started writing, and what I thought would take a few hours took several days. I gathered my collection of hand-written notes, typed them up, and put them in a dime-store binder. I walked to the garage and slid it under the front seat of the station wagon.

"A few days later his mother and I helped him move into his new dorm room. When he was all settled in, I asked him to come with me to the parking lot. It was time for the presentation. I reached under the car seat and, with words to the effect that this was what I knew about living a happy and rewarding life, handed him the bound pages. He hugged me and shook my hand. It was a very special moment."

So begins H. Jackson Brown, Jr.'s introduction to his *Life's Little Instruction Book*. And the story could have ended there, too. But a few days later Brown got a phone call from Adam, who was by now entrenched in college life at the University of Tennessee.

"Dad," Brown quotes his son as saying, "I've been reading the instruction book and I think it's one of the best gifts I've ever received. I'm going to add to it and someday give it to my son."

And suddenly the man with all of the advice was taking stock in his son's opinion. If he found value in the book, maybe other people would, too. Maybe the wisdom found within its pages deserved a bigger audience. As an advertising and marketing executive, Brown thought he might just know how to find that audience.

Within weeks, local Nashville bookstores had a few self-published copies sitting near their cash registers and on their shelves. Owners liked the format and text of the book, and they were selling steadily, but many recommended to Brown that he approach an established publisher with the manuscript. They recommended Larry Stone, publisher of Rutledge Hill Press, a small Nashville company.

Brown made an appointment to visit Stone, the two spoke briefly, though Stone told him he didn't think the project fit in with the direction the company was headed. Brown left Stone a copy of the book, anyway.

Suggestion #43 – Never give up on anybody. Miracles happen every day.

"I left that copy on my desk for four or five weeks, and everyone who came in my office picked it up, flipped through it and even read a few things out loud," Stone said. "It caught up to me one day, and I thought hey, we probably ought to reconsider this book. So I called Jack up and asked if he had found a publisher. He said, 'No', and I said, 'You have now.' "

Suggestion #123 – Learn to listen. Opportunity sometimes knocks very softly.

Rutledge Hill published the book in 1991 in paperback, with the title in black text surrounded by a plaid border. It was small, just 4 1/2" by 6", and priced at just $5.95, making it a perfect stocking stuffer, thank-you gift, housewarming present or, obviously, graduation sentiment. Sales were steady, and climbing. More than just local bookstores were taking notice of the little advice book that could.

"We had three printings in 1991," Stone said. "That June, Walden (Books) called us up and said that the book was going to be one of the year's best-sellers. 'How do you know,' I asked them. They said, 'We just have our ways. We know.' "

They did, because 1.5 million copies of the title were sold in 1992, and another 3,390,994 copies sold in 1993, according to *Publishers Weekly* figures. The book spent 52 weeks on the magazine's best-seller list in 1992, and 48 weeks on the same list in 1993. And the book was a *New York Times* best-seller, as well.

"Rutledge Hill Press has a most unusual distinction on *The Times* lists for June 21: Its *Life's Little Instruction Book* is No. 1 in the Advice, How to and Miscellaneous category in both hardcover and paperback. It appears to be the only time in memory that the same book hit the top spot simultaneously in hard and soft. . ." wrote Esther B. Fein in *The New York Times Book Review*.

Newspaper columnists devoted entire columns to the book, TV and radio talk show hosts quoted from it, bookstores across the country planted it front and center in their store windows and teachers from elementary school to college read it to their students.

"Jack appeared on *The Today Show* and Walden books sold 10,000 copies that day," Stone said, apparently still in awe of those numbers nearly four years later.

The Ad man from Nashville and his slow-to-be-convinced publisher had a hit on their hands.

"My wife and I are black and blue from pinching ourselves," Brown told *USA Today* on April 14, 1993. "Is this really happening?" He chalked the book's success up to the universal appeal it had for readers. "They hear a voice from their past – someone who cared for them – their mother's or father's."

#252 – Take good care of those you love.

Despite the book's sentimental tone and the lack of originality in many of the suggestions (many you've heard already from you own parents), many in the media even liked it. And its success led Brown and Stone to team up on other compilations, or "treasure books" as Stone calls them.

". . .They're not those ponderous tomes that make you groan at the mere sight of them," wrote Susan Watson, of *The Detroit Free Press.* "No way. Brown's offerings float on the currents of whimsy and summer-sweet memories. When they land, they gently nudge us, friends and strangers, a little bit closer to each other." And, she noted, his books, "stick to the best-seller lists like magnets to metal."

In its August 1993 issue, *Southern Living* even positioned the book as a beach read. "What better place than the beach to contemplate the mystery of life? Like eating a jar full of peanuts, you can pick these aphoristic bits of wisdom from the book just a few at a time, or by the handful."

And Sis Bowman, of the Zanesville *Ohio Times Recorder* wrote, "Every time a new H. Jackson, Jr., compilation hits the book stands, I feel as if an old friend has reappeared."

#214 – When complimented, a sincere "thank you" is the only response required.

The other titles (*Life's Little Instruction Book II, Life's Little Instruction Book III, Live and Learn and Pass it On, The Little Book of Christmas Joys*) have lead Brown to quit the advertising business and concentrate on his book projects. "He still does a little work for clients who are really good friends," Stone said. That success has also changed Rutledge Hill, bringing with it new challenges. "The real trick is that such growth doesn't destroy the company," Stone said. But despite the mega-sellers the pair have worked on at heart, Stone is still a publisher and Brown, a dad.

"I'm not really a writer, but a father," Brown told *USA Today.*

#502 – After you've worked hard to get what you want, take the time to enjoy it.

America's #1 Self Help Bestseller

L. RON HUBBARD

DIANETICS

The Modern Science of
Mental Health

New Edition for the '80s
A Handbook of Dianetics™ Procedure

7

DIANETICS

by L. Ron Hubbard

*"There is something new coming up in April
called Dianetics. A new science which works
with the invariability of physical science in
the field of the human mind. From all indi-
cations, it will prove to be as revolutionary
for humanity as the first cave man's discov-
ery and utilization of fire."*

— Walter Winchell,
  Syndicated columnist, 1949

Priscilla Presley and daughter, Lisa Marie. John
Travolta and wife, Kelly Preston. Jazz musician
Chick Corea. Actors Tom Cruise and wife, Nicole
Kidman. Singer Isaac Hayes. Actresses Karen Black, Anne
Archer, Kirstie Alley and Juliette Lewis. Football greats
Bob Adams and John Brodie. Now that is some pretty

exclusive company with more in common than just their celebrity status: All, at one time or another, have publicly acknowledged their membership in the Church of Scientology.

The controversial church was founded by now deceased author L. Ron Hubbard, and rooted in the principles outlined in his book, *Dianetics: The Modern Science of Mental Health*. Based on Hubbard's "science of the mind," *Dianetics* is nothing short of a publishing phenomenon. After more than 45 years of uninterrupted publication, 17 million copies of the book are in print and the work has been translated into 22 languages. Fully four decades after it was published in 1950, the title returned to the #1 spot on *The New York Times* best-seller list, and was awarded *Publisher's Weekly's* Century Award for appearing on that magazine's bestseller list for 100 consecutive weeks.

While improvement books come and go like so many fads, sales of *Dianetics* has increased every year the book has been in print. According to publisher Bridge Communications, of Los Angeles, the book will out-sell 95 percent of all books published this year.

What magic lies within its 600-plus pages that can account for such success? The cover copy of the latest edition states, "*Dianetics* reveals the single source of pain, unhappiness and self-doubt in your life – the reactive mind. And shows you how to get rid of it!"

And promotional materials from the *Dianetics* publisher explain, "It was a resounding success – because it answered not only man's search for inner peace and happiness, but confronted, head-on, each individual's responsibilities for his fellow man, and gave practical ways to overcome the seemingly impossible task of setting mankind back on the road to a better world."

A 1995 advertisement, part of a nationwide campaign, stated, ". . . it is more than a book. It is the world's first easily understood, practical and effective technology of the human mind - a technology that can be used by anyone to resolve the pains, fears, upsets, and unhappiness of their life."

Now that is powerful stuff, indeed. Imagine if you could erase all of the pain, fear and unhappiness from your life! Hubbard, citing years of research, travel and experimentation, believed he could teach you how to do just that.

The human mind, he said, was blocked by traumatic emotional memories which he termed "engrams." Only by returning to the moment of the trauma with a *Dianetics* counselor through a process called "auditing" could a person become "clear" or free of emotional trauma.

"It could be said that the purpose of therapy is to awaken a person in every period of his life when he has been forced into 'unconsciousness'," Hubbard wrote in the book. "*Dianetics* wakes people up. . . When the bulk of painful emotion is gone, the person is released; when the engram bank is exhausted of content, the person is cleared."

The actual auditing process as explained by Hubbard, sounds a bit like a combination of psychoanalysis and hypnotism. "The patient sits in a comfortable chair, with arms, or lies on a couch in a quiet room where perceptic distractions are minimal," he explains in the book. "The auditor tells him to look at the ceiling. The auditor says: 'When I count from one to seven your eyes will close.' The auditor then counts from one to seven and keeps counting quietly

L. Ron Hubbard

"Despite the controversy, or maybe even because of it, Dianetics continued to sell. By 1977, a decade after the release of the paperback version, 2.6 million copies were in print. Ten years after that, the total soared to 11 million. By mid-1996, the title was quickly closing in on the 20 million mark, and promoters have embraced the information age by launching a site on the World Wide Web."

and pleasantly until the patient closes his eyes. A tremble of the lashes will be noticed in optimum reverie. This is the entire routine."

Hubbard also patented a device called the E-meter, nicknamed "The Cans" which had a person hold a tin can in each hand while a galvanized wire hooked between the two ostensibly measured emotional stress. That way, engrams could be identified, and dispatched through the auditing process.

While that may sound like so much hocus pocus to the unconvinced, Hubbard's words offering up the possibility of mental control struck a resonant chord in society. When the book was published in 1950, it was released to an audience facing a troubled past and an uncertain future. Americans and Europeans alike were coming to terms with the end of World War II, women had achieved increasing autonomy after being thrown unexpectedly into the work-force, and they were reluctant to relinquish it. Men had returned home from the war to find a changed country. People were searching for the 'good life' they had been promised by earlier generations, and were coming up empty-handed, either financially, emotionally or both. The divorce rate was rising as were crime rates. And, to add to an already confused society, the reality of atomic fire power weighed heavily on everyone's mind. There was a spiritual void, and people were looking for something to fill it. For many, Hubbard's words filled the bill.

The book's cover shows an artist's rendering of a violently exploding volcano. That image was nothing short of a graphical prediction of the public's reception of the book. *The Los Angeles Daily News* ran a headline calling

Dianetics "THE BOOK" and proclaimed that it was "Taking U.S. by storm" and causing the "Fastest growing movement in the U.S."

The cliche term 'overnight best-seller' could easily have been coined to describe *Dianetics*. It arrived in bookstores on May 9, and first appeared on *The New York Times* best-seller list on June 18. It quickly moved up to #1. Over 25,000 fan letters poured in to the publisher's office and within six months there were 750 groups formed across the country to apply the techniques *Dianetics* espoused. During that same six months, Bridge Communications returned to the printer an unheard of seven times. By the end of 1950, 150,000 copies of the book had been sold, and the U.S.-based *Dianetics* groups had spread to Canada, Finland, Sweden, England, Germany, Switzerland, South Africa, Australia, Guatemala and Peru.

Hubbard, formerly best known as an author of pulp mystery novels and science fiction stories, had become an instant celebrity. Demands for training in *Dianetics* techniques poured in and audiences were clamoring for public appearances by the author. Hubbard hosted *Dianetics* meetings in his home in Elizabeth, New Jersey, and when he wasn't there he was booked in auditoriums around the country to sold-out crowds. To his audiences, the book had become a bible. The *Dianetics* movement amounted to a religion and in 1954 Hubbard founded The Church of Scientology - "the only major religion to have been founded in the Twentieth Century."

Introducing the new science-based religion, Hubbard explained, "Scientology does not ask one to strive towards higher ethical conduct, greater awareness, happiness and sanity. Rather, it provides a route to states where all this simply is, where one is more ethical, able, self-determined and happier because that which makes us otherwise has been eliminated."

"Scientology," he declared, "has accomplished the goal of religion expressed in all man's written history, the freeing of the soul by wisdom."

At its peak in the 1960s and '70s, The Church of Scientology reportedly had 6 million members and assets in excess of $280 million. *Dianetics* had sold over 850,000 hardcover copies by 1968, and was released in paperback.

And that's when the story gets just plain weird.

Hubbard reportedly continued to conduct research after the publication of *Dianetics,* and announced that he had discovered the existence of the human soul, or "Thetan," which had been reincarnated into various life forms for thousands of years. Those Thetans accumulated innumerable engrams along the way, which could only be removed through auditing. As demand for those auditing services increased, Hubbard sold licenses to entrepreneurs seeking to operate local "franchise" Scientology churches, requiring each to tithe back home 10 percent of its income.

"For Scientologists, truth became stranger than science fiction," reported *Time* magazine in 1976. "Hubbard's explanation of why someone might have difficulty crying: he was once a primordial clam whose water ducts had been clogged with sand." Hubbard asserted that he himself had lived through a series of incarnations and was 74 trillion years old.

In 1966, after being investigated by the Internal Revenue Service, Hubbard and 500 of his "closest" Scientology friends moved aboard a 330-foot converted British Ferry, the Apollo. The boat remained solidly in international waters after England banned foreign Scientologists, Australia revoked Scientology's status as a religion and a court in France convicted Hubbard of fraud in absentia.

Despite the controversy, or maybe even because of it, *Dianetics* continued to sell. By 1977, a decade after the release of the paperback version, 2.6 million copies were in print. Ten years after that, the total soared to 11 million. By mid-1996, the title was quickly closing in on the 20 million mark, and promoters have embraced the information age by launching a site on the World Wide Web (http://www.Ironhubbard.org). Available in five languages, the site offers visitors a staggering 30,000 pages of text and 5,000 photographs and graphics highlighting Hubbard's work.

Using computer technology to tout *Dianetics* seems an appropriate device, considering a quote from the first edition of the text; "Everyone owns the most sophisticated computer in existence – the human mind. Yet no owner's manual existed (before *Dianetics*) to unleash the mind's true power and capability."

"Where there is an open mind,
there will always be a frontier."

– Charles F. Kettering

LOVE YOU FOREVER
WRITTEN BY ROBERT MUNSCH
ILLUSTRATED BY SHEILA McGRAW

8

LOVE YOU FOREVER

by Robert Munsch

*"... he should write as if he were recording
one of his performances. This made his writing sound more spontaneous and fun to read
out loud. Munsch required a lot of feedback
from his young audience, too. Only the tales
that the children requested to hear many
times were, he felt, good enough to publish."*
– Contemporary Authors

In 1986, a new children's book was about to be published, but it needed a cover illustration. The illustra-
tor, author and publisher finally decided upon the perfect image – a diapered toddler, sitting on a tiled bathroom
floor next to an open toilet strewn with half-soaked toilet
paper. The kid is holding a wristwatch, ready to drop it in
the toilet bowl, and has obviously already had a go-round

93

with a tube of multi-colored toothpaste, some mineral oil
and a tin of talcum powder. Would you buy such a book to
read to your kids?

More than 9 million people have, sending the title to the
coveted #1 spot on the children's section of *The New York
Times* best-seller list. The book is *LOVE YOU FOREVER,*
by Robert Munsch, distributed by Canada-based Firefly
Books, and its reassuring but quirky story just plain and
simply makes kids feel OK about growing up.

> "I'll love you forever,
> I'll like you for always,
> As long as I'm living
> my baby you'll be."

That's the repeated song the devoted mother sings to her
son, no matter how big he gets – nine years old, a teenager,
a single man living across town. The clincher for parents
reading the story aloud to their children comes near the
end, when the son is grown with a daughter of his own. The
mother tries to rock him and sing him the song, but she's
too old, and too sick, so the son goes to her house, cradles
her in his strong arms and does the rocking and the
singing. Then the son goes home and lovingly rocks his
infant daughter, singing the same song to her.

After reading it through a couple times, it's tempting to
hum the verse to yourself, over and over, a bit like some
secret parenthood mantra. It's just the kind of book you'd
like to read to Scrooge, the Grinch, the Wicked Witch of the
West and your meanest elementary school teacher all
together at story-time, just to see if they really had

beating hearts after all.

The title is "quieter and more introspective" than Munsch's books, writes Andre Gagnon in *CM: Canadian Materials for Schools and Libraries* and "more ambitiously produced" said Sara Ellis, of *Horn Book.* Munsch's previous books featured loud shadow-eating monsters (*The Dark*), a sloppy, plotting mud puddle (*The Mud Puddle*) and a subway station mistakenly built in a child's living room (*Blackberry Subway Jam*). For a 51-year-old man, this guy has an uncanny child's fascination with such disagreeable topics as farts, underwear and "going pee" - making him great fun with all kids and grudgingly accepted by parents.

In *The Fart* (yet to be published), Munsch tells how the main character, Jule Ann, finds a great big purple, green and yellow fart lying on her bed. "The kids go absolutely bananas. The parents? Eighty percent think it's really neat; the other twenty percent ask, 'How could you?' " he told *Contemporary Authors.* Describing his unconventional children's stories as "middle of the road taboo" Munsch told *CA,* "Farts are perfect: you're not supposed to talk about them, but they're not very threatening."

That description – middle of the road taboo – is also an apt one for *LOVE YOU FOREVER.* Not too many children's books show pictures of aging moms cradling their grown sons in their arms, especially while sitting on their son's beds. But while the image may make some parents a bit uncomfortable, it's a reassuring one for kids. It's not quite so daunting a task to grow up when you know your mom will still be with you, still take care of you, still love you.

Love You Forever

"I . . . made the mistake of taking a part-time job in a day-care center," he wrote in Canadian Children's Literature. *"I liked the kids better than anthropology. Maybe that was because I came from a family of nine children."*

And, there really isn't a thing conventional about the way Munsch became a best-selling author, either. The son of an attorney father and homemaker mother, as a young man he had planned to enter the Roman Catholic priesthood, and later studied to become an anthropological missionary.

But the very specific road map of life that Munsch had carefully unfolded took a big detour and, thankfully for his devoted readers, never made it back to the main road.

"I . . . made the mistake of taking a part-time job in a day-care center," he wrote in *Canadian Children's Literature*. "I liked the kids better than anthropology. Maybe that was because I came from a family of nine children."

Munsch also held jobs in an orphanage, a nursery school and an infant care center, and somewhere along the way discovered, quite by chance, that he had a knack for telling stories. Some of his tales became so popular with the kids, Munsch's co-workers memorized them so when they went home at the end of the day, they could re-tell them to their own children.

But it wasn't until he took a job as an assistant professor at the University of Guelph, in Guelph, Ontario, that he tried putting his oral tales down on paper. And it wasn't his idea. His boss in the Family Studies department at the university suggested it to him. Even then, Munsch says only those stories kids had clamored for over and over were worthy of publication.

And his first efforts were lackluster, unable to recreate the mood of live story-telling until he began to write as if he were in front of an audience. This is probably why his stories seem so spontaneous, and why kids ask parents to read them again and again. It's as if the actual printed book adds little to the story except pictures, making it just the easiest most economical way to get his stories told to the most number of people. You can't help but think that if he could be in every kid's home at bedtime or storytime, sharing *LOVE YOU FOREVER* with them himself, he would.

"I figured out once that the stories the children kept requesting came to two percent of my total output," he told *Contemporary Authors*. To date, that two percent has added up to 27 published titles. And today, Firefly is confident enough in the writer's name recognition and his ability to entertain children and their parents, that the publisher opts for a standard 100,000-copy first printing with Munsch's new titles.

"Munsch's stories are mainly of contemporary, urban, domestic life, with a large dash of extravagant fantasy," *Horn Book* contributor Sarah Ellis told *CA*. "They reflect a jaunty belief in the power of children. His protagonists. . . are strong, confident and full of initiative." These are characteristics that children admire and parents seek to instill. Partly because of his ability to develop capable, clever and strong-willed characters, the Canadian Booksellers Association awarded him its highest honor, Author of the Year, in 1991. He has also received a Canada Council grant and a Ruth Schwartz Children's Book Award from the Ontario Arts Council.

LOVE YOU FOREVER is essentially the story of how a little boy becomes a man. But it is also the story of the enduring nature of parents' love and how it crosses generations. And though many other children's authors have written on that same theme, none have touched a chord in book buyers in quite the same way before or since.

Despite his success as an author, what Munsch likes to do best, and quite possibly what he is best at, is telling stories in front of live audiences. In the mid-1980s his talent as a performer was so sought after, he was booked in auditoriums seating audiences as many as 3,000 people.

But the grueling schedule of writing and publishing and speaking became too hectic, and the author has since returned to telling his well-loved stories to smaller, more informal audiences. Munsch has been known to show up in libraries and schools, sometimes with no forewarnings, introducing himself and just asking to tell some stories.

UPDATED 2ND EDITION
Over One Million Copies Sold!

The Wealthy Barber

Everyone's
Common-Sense
Guide to
Becoming
Financially
Independent

"...quite simply the best financial self-help book."
—Money Book Club, Book-of-the-Month Club

David Chilton

9

The Wealthy Barber

by David Chilton

"It should be mandatory reading."

– Paul Harvey

He's not a barber, and he doesn't like talking about being wealthy (though by most anyone's standards, he is).

He is David Chilton, guru of money management, author of *The Wealthy Barber* and mastermind behind a Canadian self-publishing empire. He is also the president of a consulting firm specializing in teaching financial planning, the host of a PBS show with the same name as the book, a sought-after public speaker, and younger than you'd expect.

He's only 34.

And about the money?

"Oh sure, financially it's been very rewarding," he said. "But because it was such an overwhelming success, I don't really have the time (to spend it). I bought a new house, but I would have done that anyway because kids were coming along. I bought a new car, but now it's five years old."

What he does like talking about is publishing.

"I'm getting a little bored with the financial planning subject," he said. "My actual love has become publishing. I like speaking, publishing, arranging for media coverage and I really enjoy sales. All of the things that most authors don't like to do, I do like to do. Over the next six to 12 months, I'm going to be looking at publishing other people's books."

And it all started in 1985 with, of all things, the Canadian Securities Test. That's the test that college grads have to take, and pass, in order to become legally-sanctioned accountants, stock brokers and security traders in Canada. Its doom-like reputation approaches that of the bar exam in the U.S., and thousands of jittery twenty-somethings take the test each time it's offered.

"Seven thousand people took the test at the same time I did, and I finished number one," Chilton said. "That gave me instant credibility. Magazines were asking me to write articles, and that was how I got my first taste of writing."

And writing, if you're to believe Chilton, made taking the Securities Test look like opening a savings account. As every writer who has taken a serious stab at a book knows, putting words on paper isn't anything but a lot of hard work. And Chilton didn't particularly care for it. But with work ethic to spare, Chilton buckled down, and started to write the book.

"I was watching *Cheers* (the television show), and it occurred to me that using humor was an effective way to bring about fairly dry ideas," Chilton said, explaining the inspiration behind the best-seller. "Why a barbershop? It gave me the ability to take the characters back once a month, and a barber is a trusted and trustworthy character."

He quit his job (he had had a string of them including stock broker, investment-firm counselor, financial planning instructor, public speaker) and worked full-time for eight months just writing and researching and rewriting.

"That's just effort," he said of the process. "That's what I'm most proud of. I can't tell you how many authors I've talked with that have told me they wrote their non-fiction book in three weeks. That's just not enough time to do a good job. I spent eight months writing full time to finish *The Wealthy Barber*. To tell you the truth, I didn't enjoy it that much. It's hard, hard work. It's brutal."

But at some point, it's over. And when Chilton finished his book, and re-read it from start to finish, he was relieved, proud, exhausted and inspired. But also a little perplexed. Who was this sappy narrator who told bad jokes, and knew nothing of money? And how about the barber, Roy? Where did this unsophisticated guy come from?

"It was not my humor at all," Chilton said, of the book's tone. "I don't even think it's that funny. What I came to realize though, is that it's the character's humor. And I think that is part of what makes the book effective."

He said that as he was writing the book, he was very concerned about information overload, and worked hard to be

David Chilton

"I'm getting a little bored with the financial planning subject," he said. *"My actual love has become publishing. I like speaking, publishing, arranging for media coverage and I really enjoy sales. All of the things that most authors don't like to do, I do like to do. Over the next six to 12 months, I'm going to be looking at publishing other people's books."*

sensitive about the amount of information the average reader could retain after finishing the book. That is the main reason the narrator starts out being very naive. The book is targeted toward people who don't know a lot about financial planning, but want to learn. So it was crucial that the narrator was unthreatening.

So finally, the book was done. But instead of racing to a publisher, Chilton bowed to a steadfast rule for the release of almost any new product. He market tested it. He gave copies of chapters out to his friends and family to read. He gauged their reactions, made some changes, and gave them back the new versions to read a second time. He gave copies of the entire manuscript to the presidents of two different major mutual fund companies, for their input.

"Both said they really liked it, but that it wouldn't sell because consumers wanted workbooks," he said. "Deep down I thought they were wrong."

And he continued on with the project. He couldn't afford a professional editor, so he made a deal with his sister (who had advanced editing and language skills) to edit the book in exchange for ten percent of the profits. He repeatedly asked his father, whom he described as a "language master" for advice on style and content. And he continued to market test.

"You should market test every product, but books are the one product that are almost never market tested," he said. "I've told this to several publishers, but they still don't market test their books. I don't understand why. That was the way we knew we had something good. It's really made us. If we wouldn't have done it, we would have released a completely different book."

In 1989, Chilton released the book in Canada. To publish it, he cashed in all of his investments, borrowed a little money, and had 6,000 copies printed. They sold in a week. Chapters (a Canadian bookstore chain) bought several thousand copies, after he pitched the book himself to a store buyer, and the remainder were bought by a Canadian financial company.

"I thought, 'Hey, this is easy.'"

But that year, he sold 25,000 copies. Not bad, considering that his original goal was to sell 10,000 the first year. But after the success of the first printing. Chilton decided he needed to approach selling the book in the same way he had writing it, and threw himself into promoting it full time.

"All I did was interviews," he said. "I did hundreds and hundreds of interviews. I averaged 170 flight days a year. And I wrote the book right at the time the market demographics dictated that a financial book would do well. My timing couldn't have been better. That was luck."

By the second year, 1990, Chilton was selling 10,000 to 15,000 copies a month.

"Most publishers have a front-list mentality," he said. "They put all their sales efforts into the first six months the book is out. That doesn't give you enough time for word of mouth to help. Make your readers your marketing team. Stay focused on the project for at least two to three years."

By the third year the book was on the Canadian bestseller list, great reviews poured in, his sister was probably the highest paid editor in the country and everyone wanted to know where David Chilton got his hair cut. He declined to reveal that secret, but good-naturedly denied that it was at a secret barber shop.

But he was quite willing to reveal his own secret to his publishing success, in the form of advice to other would-be self-publishers. A trend, by the way, he predicts will only increase, with the advance of desk-top publishing and increased esteem for small and self publishers.

"If you really want your book to fly, you need to know that the reality of the publishing business is that publishers print and distribute," Chilton said. "The author has to be willing to promote the book, because no one else will. You have to take the onus on yourself. You have to. You should cut the most aggressive deal possible, because you are the one that's going to be doing the work."

The Wealthy Barber has currently sold a million copies in Canada and 500,000 in the U.S. It is number four on the Canadian bestseller list, despite being published eight years ago. It is the bestselling book in Canadian history, outside of the Holy Bible. And, by the time the book was released in the U.S., Chilton was hosting a PBS Television show, had published *Wealthy Barber* calenders and was booked for over 75 speaking engagements.

"I've got people, adults, that tell me all the time that it is the only book they've read in years," he said, incredulously.

Chilton currently gets 250 unsolicited books a year from people wanting him to publish them. He's taken on one project, *Looneyspoons,* a cookbook by two women. Ganet Publishing Co. is the company he started to publish it, and it has been released in Canada and will be out in the U.S. He continues to get fan mail for *The Wealthy Barber,* most notably on the subject of life insurance.

"Two separate women have written to say their husbands were killed in car accidents, and that they had enough life insurance because of reading *The Wealthy Barber*. It's tragic and rewarding at the same time."

But despite its best-selling success, don't expect *Son of Wealthy Barber*, or *Wealthy Barber II*, or *A Second Haircut From the Wealthy Barber* to appear on bookstore shelves any time soon.

"I have no intention of writing a second financial book," Chilton said. "I don't know if I could do a better one. I've seen a lot of authors that come out with a second book right away, and the second one isn't usually very good. The third one stinks."

"I expect to spend the rest of my life in the future so I want to be reasonably sure what kind of future it's going to be. That is my reason for planning."

– Charles F. Kettering

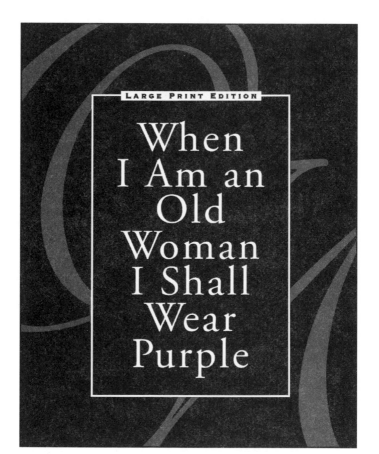

LARGE PRINT EDITION

When I Am an Old Woman I Shall Wear Purple

10

When I Am an Old Woman I Shall Wear Purple

edited by Sandra Haldeman Martz

"The literary quality of these stories and
poems is consistently high. Many of the
pieces are exciting glimpses into the lives of
old women."

– *Women's Review of Books*

When Sandra Haldeman Martz asked friends and colleagues for advice on the poetry collection she was compiling that would address women facing old age, this is what she heard:

"Nobody cares what a bunch of old women have to say."

And,

"The title is too long."

And,

"Don't show a drawing of an old lady on the cover, it'll turn people off."

111

But Martz has a great sense of humor, and she's had a few good laughs over how wrong that advice turned out to be. She has something else, too. Convictions. And what good are those, without the guts to stick to them?

After working on the project for about a year, in September 1987, Martz published 3,000 copies of *When I Am an Old Woman I Shall Wear Purple*. It is now nearly ten years later, and she just returned to the printer for the 42nd time, bringing the total number of copies of the title in print to 1.5 million. Apparently, there are a few people out there who are interested in hearing what old women have to say.

"I had published some small chap books (hand-made books, usually stapled together), and I had a sense that I was good at it," Martz said. "But I wanted to do a real book. A bookstore book. Coincidentally, about that same time I had been having a lot of real long two-bottle-of-wine conversations with my girlfriends about getting older. Here were really competent, really beautiful women and they were looking into the future and saying 'There's no place for me.'"

When I Am an Old Woman I Shall Wear Purple proved that place existed, or that if it didn't, women could create such a place for themselves. Although the phenomenal sales of the title has enabled Martz to build a successful publishing company (Papier-Mâché Press of Watsonville, Calif.) what makes her proudest is the change in society's attitude toward older women, since the release of the book.

"At the risk of being immodest, we have really been a catalyst for rediscovering how we deal with aging," she said. "In four to five years the book transformed the image of aging, which, in the public and the press, really was a negative one. And, it's caused people to re-evaluate the way we treat the elderly."

Martz's definition of the word papier-mâché is, "the art of using common everyday materials to create articles of great strength and beauty." It became her press's tag line, and even more significant, its mission statement. With the success of her first title, Martz had achieved societal change, best-seller status, and a publishing company which has since released 35 titles and employs 16 people. Not bad for a middle-aged, middle manager who left behind her 20-year career in the aerospace industry at TRW to edit poetry books.

To understand her gutsy entrance into the publishing world, Martz said you also have to understand what the climate was like in her former job. In the late 1980s the entire aerospace industry was experiencing lay-offs that exceeded 40 percent of the work force in some companies. Martz, a manager of a 200-person department, said she was beginning to feel like "just another cog in the wheel." She was entering mid-life herself, beginning to reevaluate her priorities and wanted to inject the second half of her life with profound work and meaningful relationships. She was, in her own words, "in this sort of state of flux. I was having my own mid-life crisis."

This was something that was not supposed to happen to organized, practical, logical career women in charge of their lives and their destinies.

"In my life I was seldom without a career goal and a written plan that would take me through a least the next ten years," she said. "When the corporate career path I had

Sandra Haldeman Martz

"At the risk of being immodest, we have really been a catalyst for rediscovering how we deal with aging," she said. "In four to five years the book transformed the image of aging, which, in the public and the press, really was a negative one. And, it's caused people to re-evaluate the way we treat the elderly."

chosen began to feel like a dead end, I realized that if I went through my usual goal-setting process, I would be limiting my choices to what I could imagine based on what I had already experienced. What I really wanted was something transforming."

While still working full-time at her 'real' job, Martz had collected poetry and stories from women who were also seeking to find joy in growing older. She advertised in literary magazines, newspapers and newsletters for submissions, and *Coda,* the magazine then published by Poets & Writers Inc. Within a few weeks, her mailbox overflowed with responses. The quantity, and quality, of the work she received were her first indication that her idea was going to be a popular one. She had hit a nerve. It was one that had been exposed for quite awhile, but gone unnoticed.

"Seven hundred to eight hundred submissions came to my house," she said. "They were on all different kinds of paper. Some were handwritten. There was nothing formal about them. None had recognizable names. But you could feel the emotion on each page. The intensity of the material was overwhelming."

Some, she openly admitted, made her cry. Some made her nod her head in agreement. Some were funny and some even ticked her off, but she was suddenly the trustee of a quantity of priceless, diverse, personal writings on aging, written by women raised in a culture that values youth over almost everything else.

But regardless of the emotion they evoked, all made her committed to publishing the book, and giving the writings a public forum. Commitments are admirable, but printing, binding, cover designs and marketing all cost money. Lots of money. Haldeman had no secret investor waiting in the wings to pay the bills, no multi-million dollar publishing company to ease the project into its budget. What she did have was excellent personal credit from her years as a well-paid manager. Have credit cards, will self-publish. Martz put the bills on her plastic.

"I basically financed my business with credit cards," she said. "Can you believe that? But I was very focused and very committed to the project. I knew it would work. I just flatly refused to let anything sway me from trusting my instincts."

She charged printing bills, binding bills, advertising bills, all at 21 percent interest. That unsecured debt was backed up with only her belief in the project, and the hunch she would be able to sell books.

"What is entering the public's consciousness these days? I'm always trying to understand and pay attention to that," she said. "At that time, aging was very much in the public consciousness but it was not addressed in an easily-accessible and literary format. I had that with this book, and its time had come."

The title of the collection came from the first line in a poem, *Warning,* submitted by Jenny Joseph. The first stanza of the poem reads:

"When I am an old woman I shall wear purple

With a red hat which doesn't go, and doesn't suit me.

And I shall spend my pension on brandy and summer gloves.

And satin sandals, and say we've no money for butter.

I shall sit down on the pavement when I'm tired

And gobble up samples in shops and press alarm bells

And run my stick along the public railings

And make up for the sobriety of my youth.
I shall go out in my slippers in the rain
And pick the flowers in other people's gardens
And learn to spit."
Something about those words, and the others in the book, reverberated from woman to woman, and within six weeks, Martz had sold out of the first printing of 3,000 copies. She went back to the printer twice that year, selling all 9,000 copies of the book she had printed, with only word of mouth for advertising.

According to her figures, in 1988 Papier-Mâché, with only that single title, grossed $60,000. In 1989, that figure rose to $100,000, in 1990, $300,000 and in 1991, after winning an American Booksellers "Book of the Year" honors award, sales of the book grossed $1 million. According to *The Los Angeles Times,* Papier-Mache grossed $3.6 million in 1993, turning a 20 percent pretax profit.

And unlike some of the other titles profiled, book reviewers generally loved the title.

". . . it sounds a message, addressing a group that needs and wants to hear it."
-L.A. Times

"How do you account for an underground best seller on the subject of aging women? The answer is easy: honesty. This is a small-press runaway success about older women as we really know them. . . The book is finely crafted, unusual in its focus, universal in its ability to sensitize us to the human condition."
-Georgia Journal

"An important, moving, and life-affirming book. . . The various works speak about dignity, about respect, and about caring. About saying good-bye to old friends and hello to new ones. . . About not growing old gracefully, if that's what suits you."
        -*Reading for Pleasure*

"You're not getting older, just a little more purple."
        -*Milwaukee Journal Sentinel*

The success of the book presented Martz with the opportunity – and the challenge – of a lifetime. She quit her job, moved to northern California, and became a full-time publisher.

"It was an anxiety-ridden decision," she said. "But I had this unshakable belief that it would all come together. I could see that there was a need for the kind of books that I wanted to publish."

In 1991 Martz realized Papier-Mâché had grown beyond her abilities to run it alone, so she hired a full-time staff person to help with marketing the book. But she was still about as 'hands-on' as you can be in publishing.

"I continued to do all the shipping and billing, can you believe that?" she laughed. "I don't ship and bill anymore. I've arrived!"

She had indeed, and her success had not gone unnoticed by a few of the larger publishing companies. She was presented with several lucrative offers from large publishing companies who wanted to buy the rights to sell the title. Martz was flattered, but uninterested.

"I really can't even remember how much they were for or who they were from," she said. "I never even seriously considered a one of them."

Papier-Mâché and *When I Am an Old Woman I Shall Wear Purple* had infused her life with the meaning she felt had been lacking. She had developed personal relationships with the women who had shared their intimate stories with her. And, she had discovered a wealth of unknown talent – every publisher's brass ring. Self-publishing had claimed another devotee. She was hooked.

"I felt like I would have just been giving away my key asset," she explained. "Our readers are our writers. I don't know of any other publisher that can say that. If I had sold the rights, who would have taken care of them?"

Martz takes that role of nurturer/friend/editor seriously and has since worked with many of the contributors to the first book on many other projects. She has also proven that the success of her first "bookstore book" wasn't a fluke. The sequel to her best-seller was, *If I Had My Life to Live Over I Would Pick More Daisies*. It sold over 350,000 copies in its first year in print (1992). A third anthology, *I Am Becoming the Woman I've Wanted,* has sold over 125,000 copies and won the company's second American Book Award.

Her latest release is *Grow Old Along with Me – the Best is Yet to Be* another anthology. But this time when the call went out for submissions, Martz received 7,000 answers, instead of 700. The title also features fiber artist Deidre Schrer, whose work appeared on the cover of *When I Am an Old Woman I Shall Wear Purple* and four other subsequent Papier-Mâché books. Martz has also published

---

Threads of Experience, a four-color collection featuring Deidre Scherer's fabric and tread art *Like a Summer Peach: Sunbright Poems and Old Southern Recipes,* co-edited by Janice Townley Moore, also a contributor to *When I Am an Old Woman I Shall Wear Purple.*

Although it may be rare to find a person with both a big, caring heart and crack-shot business sense, that is probably the key to Martz's ground-breaking success. While supporting and encouraging writers, managing a growing staff and developing a well-deserved reputation as a quality literary publisher, Martz has not lost sight of her potential to be successful financially. Papier-Mâché is the envy of many small publishing companies for its savvy use of sidelines, or book-related products. The company makes a healthy profit selling T-shirts, posters, mugs, tote bags and even aprons with favorite images and quotes from the company's books printed upon them.

These products were developed to respond to an almost cult movement among some older women to celebrate 50th birthdays with "purple parties."

"Used to be when a woman turned fifty someone would throw an 'Over the Hill' party for her," explains the text in the company's fall 1996/spring 1997 catalog. "She'd probably get annoying presents like golf caps that say 'I'm only seven years old in dog years!'. . .(Instead) All her friends will gather together wearing purple dresses and red hats, and she'll receive gifts like mugs that say 'I Love Purple' or a copy of the book *When I Am an Old Woman I Shall Wear Purple. . .* Women across America have taken the message of Martz's best-selling anthology to heart – it's OK to grow older; in fact, it's terrific!"

The next Martz anthology will continue to explore Papier-Mâché's now well-known theme of aging, but will focus on intergenerational relationships. If her past success is any indication, she can only be viewed as a living example of that oft-quoted but seldom-believed cliche, 'everything gets better with age.'

WHAT TO EXPECT WHEN YOU'RE EXPECTING

A pregnancy guide that reassuringly answers the concerns of mothers- and fathers-to-be, from the planning stage through postpartum.

Clear, comprehensive month-by-month format.

❖

By Arlene Eisenberg, Heidi Eisenberg Murkoff, and Sandee Eisenberg Hathaway, R.N.

❖

With a foreword by Dr. Richard Aubry, Director of Obstetrics, Upstate Medical Center, Syracuse, NY

11

WHAT TO EXPECT WHEN YOU'RE EXPECTING

by Arlene Eisenberg, Heidi Eisenberg Murkoff
and Sandee Eisenburg Hathaway

"The first thing you should buy after the
pregnancy test comes back positive!"
– Sally Wendkos Olds, co-author
The Complete Book of Breastfeeding

You would be hard-pressed to find an obstetrician's waiting room that didn't have at least one dog-eared copy. And you'd eat a lot of cake and drink a lot of punch before you found a baby shower where there wasn't a brand new one carefully wrapped in blue and pink paper. A pregnant woman can recognize it at 500

Arlene Eisenberg

As of June 1996, Workman had sold over five million copies of the original book, and at least that many of all of the spin-off titles. With the tired and over-used comparison of writing a book and having a baby being the bane of any publishing editor's existence, here's one title fully allowed to use the cliche.

yards, and fathers-to-be have been known to devour it like it was the latest Tom Clancy thriller.

We're talking, of course, about *What To Expect When You're Expecting*, otherwise known as 'The Pregnancy Bible.'

Written by a mother and her two daughters, the book was first published in 1984, and 12 years later was listed by *USA Today* as the 27th best-selling book in the country. Arlene Eisenberg also collaborated with her husband (a surgeon) and his brother, an obstetrician/gynecologist, when writing the book.

Workman Publishing, of New York City, the company which published the title and continues to publish updated editions, has capitalized on the spin-off market, releasing *What To Expect The Toddler Years*, *What To Expect The First Year*, *What To Eat When You're Expecting* and *What To Expect When You're Expecting Pregnancy Organizer*.

As of June 1996, Workman had sold over five million copies of the original book, and at least that many of all of the spin-off titles. With the tired and over-used comparison of writing a book and having a baby being the bane of any publishing editor's existence, here's one title fully allowed to use the cliche. And, of course, the literary possibilities were just too tempting for co-author Heidi Eisenberg.

"Books and babies have a lot in common," she writes in the book's acknowledgements. "Both take plenty of time, hard work, dedication, and care (not to mention a heavy dose of worry) to turn out the best possible product."

It was the "heavy dose of worry" that lead the moth-

Heidi Eisenberg Murkoff

"I was pregnant, which about one day out of three made me the happiest woman in the world," reads the introduction. "And for the remaining two, the most worried."

er/daughters writing team to turn out the book in the first place.

"I was pregnant, which about one day out of three made me the happiest woman in the world," reads the introduction. "And for the remaining two, the most worried."

Like all pregnant women, Heidi had the standard worries: would the wine she drank before she knew she was pregnant harm her baby; was she drinking too much coffee and not enough milk; was she eating too much sugar and not enough protein. Heidi even worried when she was feeling good.

"I don't have morning sickness. . . something must be wrong!," she writes in 'How This Book Was Born.'

But although just about every woman who has ever been pregnant has harbored the same concerns, when Heidi and her sisters were pregnant, nobody was addressing them.

She writes: "Where could I turn to find reassurance that all would be well? Not to the ever-growing stack of pregnancy books piled high on my bedside table. As common and normal as a few days of no fetal activity is in the fifth month, I couldn't find a single reference to it. As often as pregnant women take a tumble – almost always without harming their babies – I could find no mention of accidental falls."

And even worse, when she could find mention of one or more of her worries, they often times were discussed only in a very serious way, alarming her even further.

"I certainly couldn't find relief for my worries by opening a newspaper, flipping on the radio or television, or browsing through magazines. According to the media,

Sandee Eisenberg Hathaway

The three women decided to take what they learned from their own experiences with pregnancy, and add to it the latest research, and write a book that would become pregnancy's voice of reason.

threats to the pregnant lurked everywhere: in the air we breathed, in the food we ate, in the water we drank, at the dentist's office, at the drugstore, even at home."

And so, the three women decided to take what they learned from their own experiences with pregnancy, and add to it the latest research, and write a book that would become pregnancy's voice of reason. No one will ever know how many calls to family practitioners and obstetricians were headed off by the publication of the book. Suffice it to say, a lot.

The book has 18 chapters beginning with 'Are You Pregnant?' and ending with 'Preparing For the Next Baby.' Do you want to know if paint fumes are bad for your developing baby? It's in Chapter 3 under 'Household Hazards.' Irritated by the unwanted advice that seems to be coming from everyone you know? Check out Chapter 8, ". . . don't let unwanted advice get your dander up. Neither you nor your baby will profit from the added tension."

However, the publication of the book might be the single exception to that rule; countless numbers of women and their families have benefitted from its publication, which was the direct result of worry and tension. Heidi writes, was ". . . out of our concerns, *What to Expect When You're Expecting* was born."

The
Macintosh
Bible™

ZILLIONS OF BASIC AND ADVANCED
TIPS, TRICKS AND SHORTCUTS,
LOGICALLY ORGANIZED AND FULLY INDEXED

Arthur Naiman, Nancy E. Dunn,
Susan McCallister, John Kadyk
and a cast of thousands

12

the
Macintosh
Bible

edited by Arthur Naiman

"The single most helpful book about the Mac. . . It's hard to find a page that doesn't have a useful tip. . . Like having a Macintosh expert at your side whenever you need one."

– New York Times

Who knew computers, or rather, writing about computers, could be funny? Only anyone who has ever owned one, worked on one, or opened up a computer manual. With the exception of the people who write those manuals, of course. Most have yet to exhibit even a hint of life, let alone a sense of humor. More often, you need a sense of humor just to read them.

But leave Arthur Naiman out of that generalization. Now that guy is funny. And opinionated. And, surprisingly enough, an author of books about computers. The combination ads up to sheer readability. Parts of his bestselling *the Macintosh Bible* read more like a compilation of essays on modern-day life in the computer age than a computer instruction book.

For an example of Naiman's humorous side, read what he has to say on software companies: "Most of them don't have the brains God gave a slice of French toast."

Or, Naiman on computerized phone systems: "Basically a form of automated passive aggression, designed to discourage every telephone call that isn't an order (you notice how rare these systems are in the *sales* departments)."

And Naiman on software manual tutorials: "They're the equivalent of being strapped into a chair and forced to listen to scales for three months, then 'Three Blind Mice,' then 'Twinkle, Twinkle, Little Star,' then Lawrence Welk – all under the guise of teaching you music appreciation."

It was Naiman's opinion of the publishing industry- "...couldn't stand how clueless and/or sleazy most publishers were (not *all*, but most)" – which led him to self-publish *the Macintosh Bible*, under the imprint Goldstein & Blair. No newcomer to the field, Naiman had already written 12 books for several entrenched publishing companies, but told *Publishers Weekly* he was fed up with "other publishers messing up my books." More specifically, he could do without editors that stripped his work of its personality and marketers that just plain didn't work hard or smart enough to boost his sales.

Naiman, 55, a self-described atheist whose politics run to the left of say, Abbie Hoffman, originally set up Goldstein & Blair to publish political books. Born in 1941 in Chicago, the son of a salesman father and a clerk/secretary mother, Naiman got his college degree from Brandeis University in 1962, and his Master's from Bank Street College in 1976. He taught both high school and junior high school in New York City, alternative high school in East Harlem, and elementary school in South Bronx. Naiman's teaching abilities made him a natural when it came to computer books and publishing.

Peter H. Lewis, of *The New York Times,* said about *the Macintosh Bible*, It's ... "like having a Macintosh expert at your side whenever you need one."

Naiman's company got its name from a character in George Orwell's classic novel *1984* (Emmanuel Goldstein was the head of the underground) and Orwell's birth name (Eric Blair). But somehow Naiman began cranking out his behemoth Macintosh tome before the political ones took shape, and Goldstein & Blair was a handy catch-all.

"The Goldstein & Blair dba ("doing business as" registration form) was just sitting there, so I used it," Naiman wrote, in *the Macintosh Bible's* introduction.

The book was received with glowing, fawning, slobberingly happy reviews and even what could be called a sense of relief. At last! Finally someone had written an interesting, secret-packed, all-inclusive but intensely readable reference guide to the most fascinating computer being manufactured today. And it gave the quirky little machine

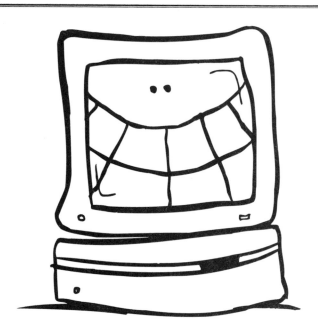

the Macintosh Bible

"...couldn't stand how clueless and/or sleazy most publishers were (not all, but most)" – which led him to self-publish the Macintosh Bible, *under the imprint Goldstein & Blair. No newcomer to the field, Naiman had already written 12 books for several entrenched publishing companies, but told* Publishers Weekly *he was fed up with "other publishers messing up my books."*

some legitimacy in the process.

"For years, many business-people treated the Mac as a toy, while those of us who'd already had a bellyful of the deranged command structure of more primitive computers romped happily in the fields of Macintosh," writes Naiman, calling the machine, "the most intuitive computer ever sold."

Writers, graphic designers, desktop publishers and managers were all having a great time using the little tan computer with the small screen and rainbow-striped apple to organize and simplify their work. Why couldn't anybody translate the near cult loyalty of these creative types into a book? That is exactly what Naiman did.

"Superb" "Excellent" "Rating: A" "A must-have" "Indispensable," read the reviews from the *Computer Book Review* to *The Mac Street Journal* to *Booklist*. Even with the daunting price of $32 for a softcover title, the *Macintosh Video News* and the *A-E-C Automation Newsletter* both called the book a bargain. Wow! I guess when the reviewers are telling you, indirectly, to raise your price you've really got something.

People want to be entertained, even while they're reading about how to get the most out of their computers, and Naiman has found that if you can do that, people will pay a fair price for your product. Within three years of publishing the first edition (there are now six), 400,000 copies of *the Macintosh Bible* had been sold, making it the best selling book ever published on Apple's flagship computer.

A "plus is the book's punchy, down-to-earth style, which makes it a pleasure to read. Although it's designed as a reference work, I found myself reading whole sections of tips at a time," wrote Charles Rubin in the *San Jose Mercury News.*

But as several of the authors profiled have found, putting out a best-selling, critically-acclaimed book has a way of creating a business around itself. Just to perpetuate sales, fill orders, update text for new editions and keep up with changes in the industry, Goldstein & Blair employed more than 20 people. Suddenly, Naiman was a businessman. A very successful businessman, but after awhile, not a very happy one. He was intensely pleased with the book's success. It was his idea, after all. And, in his own small way, he had taken on the computer giant of IBM (and their clones) and won. He wrote and edited large portions of all six editions, and was even willing to take the heat if no one laughed at his jokes.

"Regardless of who wrote the original drafts (there were 43 people listed in "Credits" and 22 in "notes on major contributors"), I rewrote them with a very heavy hand, to try to make the whole book speak with one voice (mine, for better or worse). If the jokes aren't funny, that's my fault too." Naiman himself is listed in "Credits" as being in charge of "Editorial supervision, hysterics and jokes."

Rest easy Arthur, you're funny.

But success strained his sense of humor. Naiman was finding out that he didn't have time to write or publish political books; that the more successful the company got, the less he had to do with writing and editing (which he loved) and the more he had to do with managing and number crunching (which he didn't).

"Although Goldstein & Blair was very good to me financially, I felt enormously burdened by the effort it took to run it, and by not having time to do anything else," wrote Naiman. It seems that even he had partially forgotten the first of his own Ten Commandments of using computers: *"This is the Mac. It's supposed to be fun."*

With the slightly skewed idea that politics is what's really fun, Naiman made a deal in 1992 with Peachpit Press of Berkeley, Calif. to distribute *the Macintosh Bible* and all of Goldstein & Blair's other titles. Subsequent editions of the best-seller were written and edited by Naiman and his gang, but published by Peachpit. "After years of tearing my hair out (and you thought it was male pattern baldness), I'm delighted that. . . the . . . people at Peachpit. . . are taking the burden of publishing off my shoulders."

"Having made a success of writing (and now publishing) computer books – something I fell into almost by accident – I want to transfer my skill at making complicated subjects accessible (and even more enjoyable) to the area of politics. If the left's main stock in trade is the truth – and if it isn't, what hope is there?- then the left's main job is education. Yet most leftists talk to the already converted, in language (and with a design sense), that only the already converted will put up with. I think there's a much wider audience for political truths, and I'm going to try to address it."

The One Minute Manager

The Quickest Way to Increase Your Own Prosperity

Kenneth Blanchard, Ph.D.
Spencer Johnson, M.D.

A GEM!
"Whether you
manage a home,
a business,
or a family it
works."

0-425-06265-1 · $6.95 · IN CANADA $7.95 · A BERKLEY BOOK

13

The
One
Minute
Manager

by Ken Blanchard

"One of the more unusual books on the
bestseller list!"
– *New York Times*

In 1982, $15 was a lot of money. It could take a family of four out to dinner, pay the monthly electric bill, buy a new pair of Calvin Klein jeans (if they were on sale) or get you and a friend two tickets to a Madonna concert.

In 1982, $15 could also buy a skinny little 100-page book on organizational management. Organizational management? Despite the hefty price tag, and the seemingly esoteric subject matter, the book became a bestseller and

Ken Blanchard

*"Once there was a bright young man who was looking for
an effective manager. He wanted to work for one. He wanted
to become one. His search had taken him over many years to
the far corners of the world. He had been in small towns and
in the capitals of powerful nations,"* begins the story of The
One Minute Manager.

launched a successful writing and speaking career for its author, Dr. Ken Blanchard.

The originally self-published title was picked up by Berkley Books and released in arrangement with William Morrow and Co., Inc. The company has sold more than 12 million copies of the book, and Blanchard has become an internationally known author, educator and consultant. He is chairman of Blanchard Training and Development, Inc., a leading management training firm based in San Diego. His words have impacted the day-to-day management of millions of people and thousands of companies, and he has gone on to write several other books. He began with one initial idea, and a good story.

"Once there was a bright young man who was looking for an effective manager. He wanted to work for one. He wanted to become one. His search had taken him over many years to the far corners of the world. He had been in small towns and in the capitals of powerful nations," begins the story of *The One Minute Manager*.

No matter how trite the description has become, especially in the business arena, Blanchard could only be described as a "people person." That is obvious from the success of his book, his status as a sought-after public speaker and his keen sense of observation which provided the basis for *The One Minute Manager*.

"In this brief story, we present you with a great deal of what we have learned from our studies in medicine and in the behavioral sciences about how people work best with other people," Blanchard writes in the book's introduction. "By 'best,' we mean how people produce valuable results, and feel good about themselves, the organization and the other people with whom they work."

First educated at Cornell University, Blanchard studied people's work styles professionally as a professor of organizational behavior at Ohio University and the University of Massachusetts and later as founder of the Blanchard Training and Development Center. But from his words, it's easy to surmise that he has a personal interest in the subject, and a talent for connecting with people.

"Life is a series of serendipitous events," Blanchard has said. "It is what happens to you when you are planning to do something else. My own life has been a series of such occurrences."

For him, that "something else" turned out to be a completely unexpected successful writing career. The story goes that despite a bachelor's degree, master's degree and Ph.D., and the countless writing assignments that accompanied them, he had never thought of himself as a particularly good writer.

"I never dreamed of being a writer because most of my professors in graduate school said my writing was not academic enough," he told *Contemporary Authors*. " I later learned that the problem they had with it was that you could understand it. The reason I really like writing is that you get immediate feedback every day as you make progress on a work. The key to the success of *The One Minute Manager* was that we used a very different approach to writing. Rather than writing as an art for our own satisfaction or the satisfaction of a few colleagues, we wrote for the satisfaction of the reader – managers all over the country."

Four different drafts of the book were written by

Blanchard and his collaborator, medical doctor Spencer Johnson. Each draft was then given to 250 to 300 people to read and critique, in what could only be called an early market test, similar to what David Chilton did with his bestseller, *The Wealthy Barber*, years later. The authors asked these market testers for suggestions on what would make it "the best book they had ever read on management." And, true to the advice given to readers in the finished book, they willingly incorporated the ideas they received.

The process worked, and after becoming a *New York Times* best-seller in 1982, *The One Minute Manager* went on to sell in over 50 other countries, and be translated into 25 languages. Blanchard has gone on to work as a consultant for the likes of Chevron USA, Eastman Kodak Company, Florida Power & Light and Builders Square. He also has written other books in *The One Minute Manager* library. They include *Everyone's A Coach*, co-written with former Miami Dolphins coach, Don Shula; *The One Minute Manager Gets Fit*; and *The Power of Ethical Management*, co-written with Norman Vincent Peale. In 1991, Ken Blanchard received the National Speakers Association's highest award, the Council of Peers Award of Excellence. He is also a visiting lecturer and trustee emeritus at his alma mater, Cornell University.

"Successful people are people that see an opportunity and know when to move," Blanchard told *Contemporary Authors*. He, of course, was describing himself.

MUTANT MESSAGE
DOWN UNDER

MARLO MORGAN

14

MUTANT MESSAGE DOWN UNDER

by Marlo Morgan

*"The story of a courageous woman, who
walked with the Aboriginals and learned the
wonderful secrets and wisdom of an old, old
tribe. Things we all need to learn in our
modern society: to get back in touch with
nature, to trust and have faith in our inner
knowledge and guidance."*
– Elisabeth Kubler-Ross

The designation in the upper left hand corner on the book's back cover reads simply, 'Fiction.'

However, in the opening section of *Mutant Message Down Under* entitled 'From the Author to the Reader, Marlo Morgan writes, "This was written after the fact and

Marlo Morgan

"People want to argue about this whole thing," she told The Chicago Tribune. *"They want to argue about did it happen, is it a figment of your imagination, give us names, what school did you go to – all that. None of that has anything to do with anything so I've finally gotten to the point where this is sold as fiction."*

inspired by actual experience."

From just that little bit of information, anyone could surmise that the lawyers have been sticking their two cents in. Not unusual in publishing, but certainly not always welcome, either.

The controversy goes something like this: If the book was to be republished by HarperCollins in 1994 as a factual account of an actual event, Morgan would have to reveal the identity of her "interpreter" – the man who became her constant guide on a life-altering spiritual and physical journey through the Australian outback. She refused. The sites she had been able to visit on her four month walkabout were fragile and sacred. The people she met had selected her to tell their stories, and did not want to be contacted by a bunch of New York publicists and fact-finders. And, she had been asked to keep a secret. And anyone who had the difficult but inspiring experiences that Morgan writes about in the book, is certainly going to have little trouble keeping a promise.

"People want to argue about this whole thing," she told *The Chicago Tribune*. "They want to argue about did it happen, is it a figment of your imagination, give us names, what school did you go to – all that. None of that has anything to do with anything so I've finally gotten to the point where this is sold as fiction."

But at the same time, this chiropractor/grandmother turned best-selling author couldn't have been too enamored with the fiction classification, after enduring such a grueling physical test. According to her book, that included being swarmed upon by flies, having her blistered feet harden into something that resembled hooves and eating some pretty unappetizing local flora and fauna.

Who could fictionalize this:

"We came across a mound of ants, big ones, probably an inch long, with strange, distended centers. I was told, 'You are going to love this taste!'"

Or would want to make up, "The air was so still, I could feel the hair growing in my armpits." Or even, "The problem was one of odor. I had become offensive. It was true. I could smell myself and see the expression from the others."

Morgan managed to swallow that bitter legal pill by giving this message to her readers:

"It appears that some people are only ready to be entertained. So if you are one of these people, please read, enjoy, and walk away as you would from any good performance. For you, it is pure fiction, and you will not be disappointed; you will get your money's ($10) worth."

"If you are, on the other hand, someone who hears the message, it will come through to you loud and strong. You will feel it in your gut, heart, head, and the marrow of your bones."

She realized that the designation also protected her, personally. According to *Publishers Weekly*, Morgan has received death threats from the likes of the Ku Klux Klan and a fundamentalist Christian group, for spreading her message of ethnic and spiritual unity. Apparently, even a best-seller can't please everyone, all of the time.

Anyway, that was how it was settled. But although it couldn't have been a wholly satisfying experience for the author, controversy is great for sales. And with 370,000 copies of the self-published book already out, HarperCollins eventually purchased the rights for $1.7 million, ordering a

250,000 copy first printing and sinking $250,000 into a marketing campaign. Part of that was spent to send Morgan on a 15-city author tour, where you can bet ants, grubs and snakes were not on the menu. And doubtless the hotel rooms had showers, and there were no crocodiles in the swimming pools!

HarperCollins has sold the foreign language rights to the title in 14 countries and it is a selection in both the Literary Guild and Doubleday book clubs.

But how did the author get from walking 1,300 miles barefoot in the Australian Outback to making million-dollar publishing deals?

Trained as a chiropractor, Morgan first went to Australia in 1985 to learn more about the country's healthcare system. There she met the Aboriginal "Real People" and made her amazing walkabout. Upon returning to the U.S., she wrote the book, looked into self-publishing, and eventually had 300 paperback copies printed in 1991. To save money, she decided not to spend the extra $700 to have the book copy-edited, even though the original text had misspelled words, typographical mistakes and all dialogue by the Aborigines was capitalized. It has since been through HarperCollins' fine tooth comb.

Reader response was overwhelming, leading Morgan to add the words, "What you hold in your hand is an original destined to become a classic," and to hit the lecture circuit. Consequently, she was so busy talking her way across her home state of Missouri, and on through Colorado and California (at $2,500 per appearance), that she was never home when, impressed with sales, the literary agents started calling.

Following a failed deal with Stillpoint Publishing of Walpole, NH, California literary agent Candice Furhman reached one of Morgan's children, who got a message to her. Furhman had purchased a copy of the book at Paper Ships bookstore in San Anselmo, Calif., and saw a big future for the self-published title. After talking with Furhman, the author agreed that it might be OK if a publisher took over distribution of the book. It was then that the deal-making began, and HarperCollins outbid all other competitors at an auction.

But though a New York City literary bidding war is a far cry from being followed by hungry dingoes through the desert in 120-degree heat, Morgan has returned to Australia four times since her first trip there in 1985. She continues to live in Lees Summit, Mo., though she travels frequently, and has donated thousands of copies of her book to schools, prisons and social service agencies. The next chapter in the story could be a Hollywood movie based on her life and her unique experiences.

Morgan, known for living modestly, told *Publishers Weekly*, "I believe I am accountable and steward for all energy that comes my way, including money."

Her interpreter, Ooota, would be happy.

"As the traveler who has once been from home is wiser than he who has never left his own doorstep, so a knowledge of other cultures should sharpen our ability to scrutinize more steadily, to appreciate more lovingly, our own."

– Margaret Mead

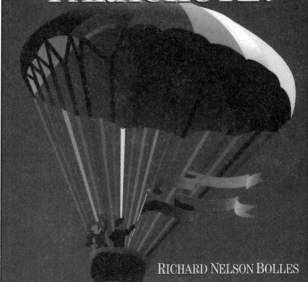

A Practical Manual for
Job-Hunters & Career-Changers

THE 1996
WHAT COLOR
IS YOUR
PARACHUTE?

RICHARD NELSON BOLLES

15

WHAT COLOR IS YOUR PARACHUTE?

by Richard Nelson Bolles

"In a domain positively viscous with lame books, this perennial best-seller has no serious competition. It is updated annually (that's impressive), it is cheery for a reader who probably could use some cheer, it has sound, detailed advice for an all-important task that is well-served with a bit of skill."

– Stewart Brand,
The Next Whole Earth Catalog

Richard Nelson Bolles has had an impressive education, a lot of jobs and more than one career. His professional life spans Harvard, the Massachusetts Institute of Technology (MIT), the Episcopal Church and San Francisco's Grace Cathedral, the U.S. Navy and membership in Mensa.

Bolles is what you might call a professional job-hunter and career-changer, and so he wrote the book on it. That's *the* book on it.

What Color Is Your Parachute? first self-published in 1972, has sold over five million copies in the last 24 years, sometimes selling as many as 64,000 copies a month. It is almost required reading for every graduating college senior in the Western world, and according to *Harvard Business Review*, "One of the finest contributions to literature on life/work planning. . ."

It started with a simple idea that grew.

"Back during one of our previous recessions, some ten years ago or more, I was struck by a thought: some people are more successful than others at job-hunting or changing careers. Why?" writes Bolles in the introduction of the 1982 edition of the book. "What do they do that the rest of us don't do? Are there any common steps or principles that seem to guide their search, from which the rest of us could learn? Coming from a family of journalists (his brother was a reporter slain in Arizona in 1976 in a celebrated suspected underworld case, and his father and grandfather were also journalists) I decided to investigate."

Bolles took the task of investigation seriously, and traveled around the country for two years, covering 65,000 miles and talking to everyone from job-hunters, to agency counselors, career experts and employment specialists.

When he completed his research, he concentrated on organizing all of the facts, statistics, anecdotes and advice into a reader-friendly format. When the manuscript was completed, Bolles said he felt enormous personal satisfaction at a job well done, but that the idea that he had completed a money-maker never crossed his mind.

"Thinking it would enjoy only a modest readership, I self-published the thing, at first," he writes. "It soon threatened to swallow up my life, in its popularity."

Apparently, there were more than just a few job-seekers and career-changers out there who were having no luck with the traditional hiring outlets, and were quick to embrace Bolles' advice. Those words of wisdom included quotes from *Cinderella* ("Fairy Godmother, where were you when I needed you?") and *Little Red Riding Hood* ("Well, yes, you do have great big teeth; but, never mind that. You were great to at least grant me this interview."), as well as statements like this one: "Let us put the matter simply and candidly: The whole process of the job-hunt in this country is Neanderthal."

Bolles was not a fan of the resume or curriculum vitae, saying they were "one of the least successful methods of job hunting that a person can use." He was fond of quoting a study that showed only one job was offered and accepted for every 1470 resumes that were received.

"I've often asked people who believe strongly in resumes or curriculum vitas if they would go up in an airplane if they knew that only one flight in 1470 would ever reach its destination!" Bolles said in an interview with Dave Jensen,

What Color Is Your Parachute?

He was fond of quoting a study which showed only one job was offered and accepted for every 1470 resumes that were received.

"I've often asked people who believe strongly in resumes or Curriculum Vitas if they would go up in an airplane if they knew that only one flight in 1470 would ever reach its destination!" Bolles said in an interview with Dave Jensen, managing director of Search Masters International of Sedona, AZ.

managing director of Search Masters International of Sedona, AZ.

Instead, his advice included telling everyone you know that you're looking for a job and the type of skills you possess, identifying your goals and objectives for a career first and then going after it and doing extensive research on the companies you would like to work for before you approach them for an interview.

His words resonated with thousands of unemployed and under-employed workers, and using his own and other's research, his book began to change the way people looked for jobs and got hired.

The sales of the book attracted the attention of publisher Phil Wood, of Ten Speed Press in Berkeley, Calif.

"The rest is history: the book went on to become what it currently is, the best-selling book on job hunting and career changing in the history of this nation," writes Bolles.

But one of the factors that keeps the book selling, year after year, has been Bolle's commitment to update it annually. Job-hunters and career-changers aren't very well armed without current information, and Bolles' text makes sure they have it. His relationship with the publisher helps, too.

Though the newspapers and publishing trade journals are ripe with author/publisher squabbles, lawsuits and the details of broken contracts, you won't hear any of that from Bolles.

"I am glad to be able to contribute a more positive model to the literature," Bolles told *Contemporary Authors.* He was especially proud of the fact that "economics are not the key consideration in the layout, but only whether or not we have produced a book as good to look at as it is to read..."

Ten Speed Press gives the author complete editorial control, editing only for spelling and typographical errors. Bolles has a unique writing style, which is part of what makes the perennial best-seller so successful. An editor could easily change that, and change the heart of the book in the process.

"As to its form: you will either love it or hate it. I was the despair of all my English teachers in college. I never learned that a preposition is something you never end a sentence with. I always started sentences without nouns, even back then. Several of my teachers became semi-suicidal, before the end of the term. I wrote as I talk. I still do."

And he continues, "The light-hearted tone of so much of the book is not intended to ignore the seriousness, indeed the wretchedness, of the job-hunt in the lives of so many today; but it is intended to make the inevitable journey a little lighter, and this book a little more enjoyable. Why should job manuals be dull? A cardinal sin, if ever there was one."

The success of the book, and Bolles' happiness in writing it is testimony to the validity of the central message in *What Color Is Your Parachute?* Investigate yourself and your professional goals intensely, put all of your effort into finding out what you want to do and into securing it. If you do what you love (Bolles loves writing), financial and personal success have a great chance of following closely.

"It's a recession when your neighbor loses his job, it's a depression when you lose your own."

– Harry S. Truman

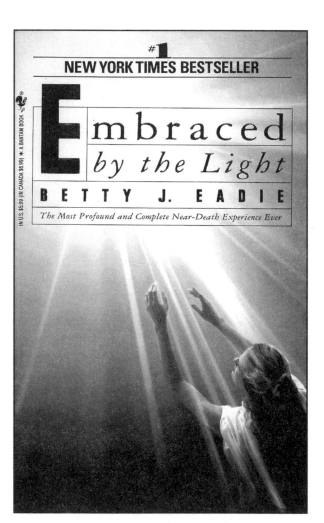

#**1**

NEW YORK TIMES BESTSELLER

Embraced
by the Light

BETTY J. EADIE

The Most Profound and Complete Near-Death Experience Ever

16

Embraced
by the Light

by Betty J. Eadie

"The most detailed and spellbinding near-death experience I have ever heard."

— Kimberly Clark-Sharp, president,
Seattle International Association of
Near-Death Studies

Wouldn't you love to have the chance to ask the following questions: What does heaven look like? Do angels exist? How about ghosts? And of course the biggie, What happens when we die?

Betty Eadie had the chance to ask them. The only catch? She had to die first. Eadie, author of the 1992 self-published best-seller *Embraced by the Light*, wrote about the near-death experience she had following her hysterectomy. According to her account in the book, after the operation and

162   INSIDE THE BESTSELLERS

Betty J. Eadie

"Then I felt a surge of energy. It was almost as if I felt a pop or release inside me, and my spirit was suddenly drawn out through my chest and pulled upward, as if by a giant magnet. My first impression was that I was free..."

alone in her hospital room, she died and came back to life four hours later. And when she returned to earth, she brought back not only the answers to the above questions, but a vivid message from the afterlife: The love you give others is the only thing of value on earth.

As far as the other questions, heaven is a garden, a city, a conference room and light show in the sky, angels are real and so are ghosts and, in her words, this is what it is like to die:

"I felt a terrible sinking sensation, like the very last drops of blood were being drained from me. I heard a soft buzzing sound in my head and continued to sink until I felt my body become still and lifeless.

"Then I felt a surge of energy. It was almost as if I felt a pop or release inside me, and my spirit was suddenly drawn out through my chest and pulled upward, as if by a giant magnet. My first impression was that I was free... I turned and saw a body lying on the bed. I was curious about who it was, and immediately I began descending toward it... That was *my* body on the bed. I wasn't taken aback, and I wasn't frightened; I simply felt a kind of sympathy for it... It was as if I had taken off a used garment and had put it aside forever, which was sad because it was still good – there was still a lot of use left in it."

That was in 1973. Twenty years later, Eadie's account of what she experienced became a *New York Times* best-seller for over 40 weeks, spending five of those in the number one spot. In May of 1993 Bantam Books paid $1.5 million for the paperback rights and that same month audio rights sold for an additional $100,000. Eadie has written a sequel, *The Awakening Heart: My Continuing Journey to Love,* published in 1996 by Pocket Books, which reportedly commanded a one million copy first printing. Death and taxes may indeed be a sure thing, but few can say they did the former and came back only to face the latter!

The huge readership she has attracted is life-times away from her initial reaction to her heavenly departure. Eadie, mother of eight children, grandmother of eight grandchildren, high school drop-out and licensed hypnotherapist, at first would only share her experience with family and friends. Upon recovery from her operation she suffered depression, anxiety and shut herself off from the outside world. It seemed that heaven was not attainable on earth.

"As the world whirled around me, I became fearful of life, even loathing it at times, praying for death. . . I became agoraphobic, fearing to leave the house," she wrote. "I remember times when I would look out the window to the mailbox and wish that I had the courage to go to it."

The encouragement of her husband, Joe, her children and her friends, as well as the adoption of a child and a visit with a "messenger" from the "spirit world" helped Eadie conquer the depression. With further coaxing Eadie told her story to the International Association for Near-Death Studies in Seattle, leading President Kimberly Clark-Sharp to call it the, "most detailed and spellbinding near-death experience I have ever heard."

According to the Christian Research Institute, of San Juan Capistrano, Calif., Eadie gave a number of talks to association-sponsored discussion groups, and in one of those an audience member took notes which were eventually passed on to Utah book editor Curtis Taylor. Taylor was so enthralled by the story that he negotiated with Eadie to publish it in book form and created Gold Leaf Press, of Placerville, Calif. just for the project. He also assisted with the actual writing of the book (the title page reads, "with Curtis Taylor") and the two forged a friendship.

"My appreciation to Curtis Taylor, writer-editor for Gold Leaf Press. Without his extraordinary talent and tremendous sensitivity to the Spirit, this book would not exist in its present form," reads the message on the first page of the book.

News Watch, a column from the *Christian Research Journal*, reports that "the book's first printing of 20,000 copies sold out within two weeks. Its second printing of 30,000 copies was snatched up just as fast. Successive printings drew a similar response and soon, waiting lists to get a copy of the supernatural saga became an ever-present dilemma for the spiritually hungry – Betty Eadie mania had struck."

Her success launched an interesting, but certainly unexpected publishing trend – putting the word "light" in book titles. Since the publication and success of *Embraced by the Light*, Signet released *One With the Light: Authentic NDEs*, by Brad Steiger and Pinnacle Books released *To Touch the Light* by Kevin D. Randle. The proliferation of 'light' titles has even led Robert Baker of the Committee for the Scientific Investigation of Claims of the Paranormal (CSI-COP) to examine the trend in an article on the organization's World Wide Web page.

"If you don't know about 'the light' then either you've been blind and deaf from birth or you are one of the sequestered jurors in the O.J. Simpson case. All other sentient beings have been exposed interminably to account after account of having died, encountered 'the light,' and returned to earth to tell about it. So many people from all walks of life have done this that we no longer have to worry about unemployment. Dying has now become one of the most popular and remunerative ways of earning a living," he writes in the article.

And there certainly are some who don't believe in Eadie's excellent adventure. Several Christian groups have accused her of being a member of the Mormon church and simply seeking to advance the Mormon faith through the book. Some criticize her theology, saying it's based on her Native American/Catholic background (Eadie is half Sioux Indian), and still others have accused her of trying to start a cult. Further detractors say she made the whole thing up just to write a best-selling book. But none of that criticism seems to be influencing her writing career. Her third book is scheduled to be released in April 1997 and she is working with a collaborator on a screenplay of *Embraced by the Light*.

And Baker, chronicler of the "light" trend, summed it up this way: " . . .all of the beings of light are in firm agreement, and they tell the dying: Stay on Earth and resist the transcendental temptation; focus on life not death; use your human powers of love and compassion in work to make this material world. . . the best world it can possibly be. This is the one thing on which all of us – the believer and the skeptic – can unanimously agree. This is the true light we all should see."

"Live as you will have wished to have when you are dying."

– Christian Furchtegott Gellert

17

How To Keep Your Volkswagen Alive

by John Muir

It was the early 1960s and the beat generation – youth who rejected the "madness" of modern society – was at the height of its popularity. Jack Kerouac's *On the Road* was jammed in the backpacks of thousands of travelers, the Beatles revolutionized popular music, American soldiers were sent to Vietnam, and though still a novelty in the U.S., the Volkswagen Beetle had been manufactured in Germany for thirty years.

It was against this societal backdrop that John Muir dropped out. A structural engineer who helped design and build NASA's Cape Canaveral, Fla. rocket launch site, Muir embraced his own version of the beats, left his job, was divorced from his wife, Irene, and grew his hair.

"He just dropped out," said Steven Carey, president of

John Muir Publications, of Santa Fe, New Mexico.
"Now this was the early sixties, so he was more of a
beat drop-out than a hippie. He drifted west and ultimately came to live in Taos. But he also liked to hang
out in Mexico, and spent a lot of his time down there.
He just did odds and ends to keep things together."

Those "odds and ends" tended to be fixing mechanical
things, most often the cars of fellow Americans, who
were making their own way through the Southwest
and Mexico. These kindred spirits of John's had also
left their lives behind and were on their own individual
adventures. Though enlightening, adventures are not
generally known to be profitable, and so these fellow
beats were doing their own "odds and ends" to pay for
food and gas. Without much money, many of them
owned Volkswagen buses or beetles or bugs. The cars
were cheap, simple and reliable, and so by default,
John Muir worked on a lot of Volkswagens. And with
that work he grew to have more than just a casual
attachment to the car. If it's possible to love an inani-
mate object, John loved Volkswagens.

"The Volkswagen has proven itself over the years to
be the best transportation buy available," wrote John,
in Chapter III of *How to Keep Your Volkswagen Alive*.
"(When shopping for a used Volkswagen) Sit in the driver's seat and scrunch your butt around. Hold the
wheel and close your eyes and FEEL!"

His admiration for the car was further reiterated in
the first chapter of the book, in a section simply entitled 'Love.'

"This is a tough one and will make or break you," he

wrote. "You must do this work with love or you fail. You don't have to think, but you must love."

But John was loving more than just cars during that time. He married and divorced a second time, and by the mid 1960s was in the midst of planning a third wedding to his final wife, Eve. Necessity intervened, and circumstances demanded he write down some directions on fixing a Volkswagen. Carey explains the story this way:

"John and Eve were going to get married, and a friend of theirs needed some work done on her bug. John didn't have time to do it, because he was busy with the wedding preparations, but he said he'd write down the instructions for the job. It was so easy, he said, any idiot could do it. That became the first chapter."

In the 25th Anniversary Edition of the book, Eve tells a similar story, of the friend who needed her bug repaired:

"Can't get around Taos without my Red Buggy. Come on John, take one last job," Debbie was pleading.

"Impossible. . . got too much to do."

"Please, John. I wouldn't trust anyone else, pleeeeze."

"Listen, Debbie, you're a weaver, good with your hands. At night, I'll type out the instructions. During the day you can do your own valve job. Use my tools and shed space," pointing to a crumbling adobe hut next to the house. "VW engines are light and easy to work on. Really. Trust yourself."

"The engine, well scrubbed, valve jobbed, got back in. Debbie connected all those loose wires, but it wouldn't start (no surprise to Debbie and me). John came to

John Muir

"The Volkswagen has proven itself over the years to be the best transportation buy available," wrote John, in Chapter *III of* How to Keep Your Volkswagen Alive. *"(When shopping for a used Volkswagen) Sit in the driver's seat and scrunch your butt around. Hold the wheel and close your eyes and FEEL!"*

adjust this and that and Debbie leaned over to watch. I was up front at the gas pedal. When the engine suddenly whirred to life, the fan belt yanked out a hank of Debbie's waist length black hair, which she tied to the engine compartment handle as a reminder. John added "compleat idiot" to the title and the wearing of stocking caps in the instructions."

And in the text of the book John added, "For months we saw that little red bug, with the pony tail flying behind it, zipping around Taos."

And so the idea of a book on how to fix Volkswagens was born. It was the fall of 1968, and John and Eve were in Mexico, planning to spend the winter there. John wrote the book over that winter, and in the summer of 1969, back in New Mexico, they conducted what may have been one of the first market tests of a book. The got volunteers with their broken Volkswagens together, read them the instructions aloud from the book, and took notes on their progress.

"We bought the parts, they did the work," Eve said.

When a school teacher who had volunteered for the mechanical experiments asked what a wrench was, the tool chapter was added.

By the fall of 1969 the book was finished, but, like many of the books profiled, no publishers were willing to publish it, saying there were already plenty of car repair manuals on the market.

"I knew there were no manuals like ours, so we sold the house in Taos, bought an old IBM composer, found a typist, and wrote to printers for bids. The plan was to sell mail order and directly to old book stores."

John and Eve had 2500 copies of the book printed that year, got in their (what else?) VW bus, drove to California and started going from bookstore to bookstore to try to sell the book. Meeting with only limited success, they eventually ran into a bookstore owner who told them they weren't going to be successful without a distributor on board to sell the title. He recommended Bookpeople in Berkeley, which was just getting started, and the two soon forged a distribution agreement. The Muirs' book and *The Whole Earth Catalog* were that company's early successes.

"After that, *Life* magazine ran a feature article on the book, and it just took off," Carey said. "But John was not a businessman, and he and Eve decided they really needed someone to manage sales. Ken Luboff ended up as John's business manager. John had met him on a beach in Mexico in 1969, and he and his wife decided to move back to Taos with John and manage the business. He just retired (from John Muir Publications) two years ago. He once told me that being the business manager meant watching the inventory, and when it got down to about 5,000 copies, calling up the printer and ordering another 100,000."

To date, two and a half million copies of the book have been sold, John Muir Publications has approximately 200 books in print and will publish 90 books this year, and employs 20 people. And, before his death in November of 1977, "John made huge sums of money on the book," according to Carey.

He and Eve bought property in Ireland, a ranch in Mexico and property in Oregon. They took their two sons on a dream vacation in Europe, and of course, expected them to know how to fix Volkswagens.

"When one of our sons became 16, John gave him our 1963 green VW van, a set of Phase I tools, an "Idiot" book, some bucks and a note To Whom It May Concern which said that he had our permission to travel," writes Eve in the 25th Anniversary edition of the book. "Explore the world" was his only instruction. From Mexico, where we were living, he drove to Florida and then started west. If I remember correctly the first phone call came from Georgia.

"Pop, the whatis has burned out."

John's answer: "Read the book."

Eve writes, "We had maybe one or two more phone calls based on VW troubles, but since the only advice John would give was, 'Read the book,' other calls consisted of 'the thingy jibbed up, but I found this really cool garage with a really helpful mechanic and. . . it's fixed.' Upon arrival in California, he could totally repair the bus, and his conception of the U.S.A. was 'the South is full of really nice people.'"

Eve continues, "That story sums up John's reason for writing the book and why I continue as its editor. It helps make people self-sufficient. We've had letters that have said things like, 'I fixed my VW, then I fixed the refrigerator, then the stove and the leaking faucet, and then. . . I built a house.' Or, 'I repaired my VW, then my mother-in-law's Ford. Once you know one car, you can pretty much fix them all." John loved letters like those."

In 1977, the same year John died, the U.S. banned

imports of air-cooled Volkswagens, citing safety concerns and emission standards. Inexplicably, the book
still sells 30,000 copies a year, according to Carey.

"I don't know who those people are, but God bless
them," he said, laughing.

"Many people know how to work hard; many others know how to play well; but the rarest talent in the world is the ability to introduce elements of playfulness into work. "

Sydney J. Harris

DEEPAK CHOPRA

THE
SEVEN
SPIRITUAL
LAWS
OF
SUCCESS

A PRACTICAL GUIDE
TO THE FULFILLMENT
of YOUR DREAMS

BASED ON *CREATING AFFLUENCE*

18

THE
SEVEN
SPIRITUAL
LAWS
OF
SUCCESS

by Deepak Chopra

"A must-read for anyone who missed The
Prophet, *by Kahlil Gibran."*
– *The New York Times*

O
n March 19, 1995, Janet Mills was sitting at her
kitchen table, all alone, screaming.

In his book *The Seven Spiritual Laws of Success*,
Deepak Copra writes, "Every cell in the human body has
only one function: to help every other cell." At that
moment, all of Janet's cells were helping her create one

179

whopper of a celebratory scream. You see the book just quoted, a book she co-published along with New World Library, had just made *The New York Times* best-seller list. And as of this writing, it has remained on the newspaper's list for 70 consecutive weeks (and has been a fixture on *Publishers Weekly's* best-seller list for eighty consecutive weeks).

"I think, as an editor, what makes an author's book a success is the energy and the conviction and the passion with which they write," said Mills, publisher of Amber-Allen Publishing, of San Rafael, Calif. "Deepak truly believes, and is passionate about, what he writes. He is also a very exceptional human being. When someone walks their talk, it really comes through in the written word."

Now "very exceptional" is usually a subjective description. Not here. Anyone familiar with Chopra's life and accomplishments would have a hard time not using those words to describe the man. He is the bestselling author of numerous books including *Ageless Body, Timeless Mind, Creating Affluence, Quantum Healing, Unconditional Life, Perfect Health* and *Return of the Rishi*. He is a world-renowned leader in the field of mind-body medicine and human potential and a respected physician and endocrinologist. He is known world-wide for his ability to blend the laws of physics with the greatest ideas in philosophy and communicate the result in plain language. He is also the former Chief of Staff at the New England Memorial Hospital in Stoneham, Mass., and has taught in Tufts and Boston University Medical schools.

By now, you're probably wondering when this man has time to write. That's not a problem, he says. He doesn't believe in the existence of time. And besides, he travels all over the world, and he writes while in flight from one time zone to the next.

"Most of my writing I do in planes, when I have plenty of time," Deepak told the *Journal of Alternative Medicine.* "I meditate whenever I have a chance."

But as far as his professional experience goes, there's more. He has collaborated with medical associations in Russia, Poland, Hungary and Brazil. He has spoken at the U.N. in New York, the World Health Organization in Geneva, the Soviet Academy of Sciences in Moscow, the Royal College of Physicians and Surgeons in Australia, and the National Institutes of Health in Washington D.C. He is the medical director of the Sharp Institute for Human Potential and Mind-Body Medicine in La Jolla, Calif., and, the item of which is possibly most proud, he has been instrumental in bringing Ayurvedic medicine (an ancient Indian healing practice) to the U.S.

Chopra is a man who has attained his own definition of professional success: ". . . the continued expansion of happiness and the progressive realization of worthy goals. . . the ability to fulfill your desires with effortless ease."

But at the same time he has refused to give in to society's obsession with that very success and what he terms the most harmful side effects of modern society, and ". . .the loss of simplicity, and the loss of trust. The experience of alienation, fragmentation, isolation. . . this leads to all of the problems, like contamination of our environment, hostility towards each other, poor nutrition, and hard work, too much work. . ."

Deepak Chopra

Chopra is a man who has attained his own definition of professional success:

". . . the continued expansion of happiness and the progressive realization of worthy goals. . . the ability to fulfill your desires with effortless ease."

In terms of his publishing life, the phenomenal sales of Chopra's books have been the vehicle for others' success as well. Most obviously, publisher Janet Mills. Though she still works from home running the company she started in 1990 (after selling her own self-published book, *Free of Dieting Forever*, to Warner Books), sometimes at that same kitchen table, things are different since the publication of *The Seven Spiritual Laws of Success*. Though those seven laws are directed at such lofty pursuits as "unity with nature" and "the seeds of divinity inside us" they seemed to have worked for Janet on more concrete concerns like banks and credit limits.

"After the book took off, financing the rapid sales wasn't too difficult. We had a credit line," she said. "Which, by the way, we don't need anymore."

Chopra's words of introduction in the book explain that the seven laws are applicable to the large and small, the known and unknown.

"Although this book is titled *The Seven Spiritual Laws of Success*, it could also be called *The Seven Spiritual Laws of Life*, because these are the same principles that nature uses to create everything in material existence – everything we can see, hear, smell, taste, or touch."

Mills is convinced these were the laws operating in sync with her own life and her own experiences, which led to the success of the book, and her own personal success. She first became intrigued by Chopra's words after hearing him speak at the American Booksellers Association convention in Las Vegas in 1989.

"I was really moved by what he had to say," she said, remembering her feelings following the speech. "The whole room was. He spoke about taking responsibility for your physical and spiritual health. At that time, my sister was dying of cancer and I was searching for ways to help her."

Seeking to explore the topic and the author further, Mills bought copies of all of his books, along with an audio tape, *Creating Affluence*. After reading them and listening to the tape, she kept having an impulse to call him or write him a letter.

"I thought his ideas were transforming, and so I was real interested to hear what he had to say about personal wealth," she said. "I listened to the tape and liked it, but as a visual person, I wanted to see it in book form. And I wanted to be the one to publish it. But I kept thinking, 'Why would he want me to do it, when he could work with any of the big companies he wanted to?'"

But the need to contact him didn't go away, and she finally wrote him a letter. Her inspiration to write it, she said, came from Chopra himself.

"His books teach you that you should follow your heart, your intuition, and do what you feel is right for you. To put the principles to work for what you are seeking."

Chopra responded shortly after that, calling her on the phone and telling her he liked the idea of the tape in book format, saying, "you came up with an idea that even Random House didn't think of."

Mills then acquired the rights to *Creating Affluence* and *The Seven Spiritual Laws of Success*, selling 50 percent interest to New World Library, also of San Rafael, Calif., which currently maintains a distribution office for the title.

To date, 1.5 million copies of the "word-of-mouth best-seller" have been sold in the U.S., with unknown foreign sales more than doubling that number. Mills is publishing other books, including one written by Chopra's son entitled *Child of the Dawn*, a parable illustrating his father's Seven Spiritual Laws in action. Chopra is currently examining research being done on Panchakarma, which is a procedure for removing toxins from the human body, to stimulate health and stave off aging and disease.

Along with Mills and Chopra himself, the rest of us "...are travelers on a cosmic journey – stardust, swirling and dancing in the eddies and whirlpools of infinity," Chopra writes in the moving conclusion to *The Seven Spiritual Laws of Success*. "Life is eternal. But the expressions of life are ephemeral, momentary, transient. We have stopped for a moment to encounter each other, to meet, to love, to share. This is a precious moment, but it is transient. . . If we share with caring, lightheartedness, and love, we will create abundance and joy for each other. And then this moment will have been worthwhile."

CONCLUSION

What is it about these 18 books? Sixty thousand books are published every year, so what magic ingredient do these titles have inside their pages that launched them to best-seller status, and turned their authors into almost instant celebrities? What universal chord did they strike in readers around the country, and the world? They've obviously got it, but what, exactly, is *it*?

For an answer, imagine all of the books profiled marinated together in a big, black kettle and melted into one giant steaming stew of words. The words melt, the stew cools, the oily liquid evaporates: What essential divined ingredient remains? The extracted quality from these titles can only be called a sense of idealism. Yes, that dogged American sense of optimism is alive, and very well, and selling books.

But several of the books profiled go beyond simple optimism, and also embrace a sense of individual spirituality, sending the message that the vibrancy of the human soul is more important than material wealth. And that is certainly a timely message, according to Gerald Celente, director of the Trends Research Institute in Rhinebeck, New York.

"Anti-materialism is definitely a major trend right now," he said. "As we all know, baby boomers are getting older and increasingly, they're asking themselves, 'What's important to me in life?'"

His Global Nomic Research he said indicates that four million baby boomers are actively focusing on the quality of their lives, rather than the rampant accumulation of possessions. There's a good chance that those same four million people have read, or are reading, several of the *Inside the Bestsellers* books. They're just the audience the authors were aiming at.

A more spiritual theme is obvious in titles like *Embraced by the Light, The Celestine Prophecy, Love You Forever The Seven Spiritual Laws of Success* and *The Christmas Box.* But even *The One Minute Manager* has an idealistic component to it, and the lessons in *Life's Little Instruction Book* include: (#43) "Never give up on anybody. Miracles happen every day" and (#332) "Live your life as an exclamation, not an explanation."

Upon closer inspection, it's almost eerie how the central message of hope and optimism can be found interspersed within the chapters of all the titles profiled here. James Redfield, are you listening? I think we're reaching, in our literary choices anyway, beyond mere coincidences. For example, Suggestion #374 on "how to live a happy and rewarding life" from *Life's Little Instruction Book* advises, "Work hard to create in your children a good self-image. It's the most important thing you can do to insure their success." Hmmm. Sounds like author H. Jackson Brown Jr. found the Eighth Insight, which Redfield describes in *The Celestine Prophecy* as "using energy in a new way when relating to people in general, but it begins at the beginning, with children. . . The worst thing that can be done is to drain their energy while correcting them."

And #438 – "Every person that you meet knows something you don't; learn from them." I guess whether he knows it or not, apparently Brown Jr. mastered the *Prophecy's* Ninth Insight, too. ". . . whenever people cross our paths, there is always a message for us. . . If we. . . do not see a message pertaining to our current questions, it does not mean there was no message. It only means we missed it for some reason."

As you read the inspiring stories herein, allow yourself the dream of writing your own best-seller. Your own great American novel, or how-to sensation, or self-help book. Use these author's experiences as a road map, a jumping-off point or even a swift kick. It's a wonderful dream to have. Hang onto it. These authors did.

Remember though, that you have to have more than just *it,* to sell books. These authors also learned the publishing business and were tireless promoters. Even after the writing process was over, they worked very hard for the luck they received. Clearly, good, consistent and long-term promotion is a critical factor in self and small published success stories. David Chilton, author of *The Wealthy Barber,* gave interviews full time for two years. And the masters of the promotion game, James Canfield and Mark Victor Hansen, authors of *Chicken Soup for the Soul,* are very proud of the fact that they never turned down an interview, no matter how unknown the publication. Betty Eadie, author of *Embraced by the Light,* and Marlo Morgan, author of *Mutant Message Down Under,* both have gone on extensive author tours, and by that I don't mean walkabouts or out of body experiences. They sold their titles on the lecture circuit.

Have you got *it?* That unknown, but instantly recognizable quality destined for bestseller-dom? There's only one way to find out, and that is by writing your book and promoting it. But take to heart *Life's Little Instruction Book's* suggestion #273 - "Remember that overnight success usually takes about fifteen years."

"The greatest thing to be gained from the reading of books is the desire to truly communicate with one's fellow man. To read a book properly is to wake up and live, to acquire a renewed interest in one's neighbors, more especially those who are alien to us in every way."

– Henry Miller

APPENDIX A

CRUCIAL Cover Design

Go ahead and judge books by their covers – everyone does it.

BY LAURA PRATT

You know the old saw, 'You can't judge a book by its cover?' Forget it. The time, thought and money invested in creating a book could be wasted if a dull or inappropriate cover causes it to get lost among the thousands of other titles in the bookstore.

"Going to the bookstore is a lot like going to the grocery store with shelves of product screaming, 'Pick me up! Pick me up!'" says Vann Baker, president of Design Etc., a graphic design company in Winston, Ga. "If something catches your eye, you have a tendency to look at it more closely. If you have to spend a lot of time discerning what the book is about, then I feel the cover design has failed."

When judging the 'book cover design' category for *Magazine Design and Production*'s Ozzie Awards, University of Oregon design instructor Roy Paul Nelson says it's not the book he's judging by its cover; it's the publisher.

"An appropriate, well-done cover gives reviewers, distributors, book-

sellers, consumers and others in the chain of the book business confidence that the publisher is serious about trying to sell a title and has a dependable business sense," he says.

Independent press publishers use both in-house and freelance designers, depending upon both the number and range of titles published in any given year. Obviously, hiring a professional is an absolute necessity. A professional cover designer will have the experience and creative ability necessary to make a book speak, loudly and clearly.

"Few authors think in graphic terms – and fewer still are well acquainted with the techniques of visual expression," says Lee Marshall in his book, *Bookmaking* (Bowker, 1965). "The book designer operates as a graphic engineer, utilizing the science and art of visual presentation to achieve optimum communication."

Selecting a Designer

One good place to start your search for a designer is at a bookstore or library. Look for book covers you like,

and then track down the designers through the authors or publishers. Contact the designers and ask them to send additional samples of their work. Once you've narrowed down the candidates, start fielding proposals. But be sure you can explain what you want.

"Most people approach it from a perspective of dollars: 'How much is it going to cost me?'" says Robert Goldstein, a graphic designer in Van Nuys, Calif., who has more than 35 years of design experience. "I try to offset that by asking them who their audience is, what they want to accomplish. Once I have determined what it is they want to do, we can talk about money, because I can design it to fit their budget."

You will find in the course of your screening process that some designers specialize in cover design, while others, such as Baker, prefer to work on the total book. "I don't see the cover as being separate from the inside," he says. "It's like when you buy a car – you're purchasing the whole package. Often the client is looking to me to

193

solve not only the creative process, but also the production process."

The designer you finally select should be someone you can get along with, says John Webster, of Abacus Graphics in Oceanside, Calif. "We spend a lot of time with our clients," he says, "and if we're comfortable together and trust each other, the time it takes to develop a good design goes smoothly."

And it should also be someone who connects with the book on an emotional level according to Fred Ramey, publisher at MacMurray & Beck, of Denver, Colo. The company publishes both fiction and non-fiction, and has made high quality book covers a priority. They've won design awards from both the Rocky Mountain Book Publishers Association and the Art Directors Club of Denver, for their efforts.

"It's important that the designer can respond to the text," he said. "That there's a reason for every element in the design."

The Creative Process

It is a designer's job to mobilize color, form, line, typography and other visual elements of the book cover "so that their sum, and each one of them, will contribute to a successful solution of the creative problem," says Marshall in *Bookmaking*. "The designer's creative problem is somewhat like that of the abstract painter – to communicate in terms that will reach the subconscious levels of the viewer's mind, where response will be automatic reaction rather than conscious thought."

Robert Aulincino, an independent book designer in New York City with more than 6,000 covers to his credit, begins the creative process by discussing with the author and publisher what the book is about and how they would like to see it presented. "I usually give more than one solution to a customer," he says. "Recently, I gave eight versions to a client. We both agreed the last design was the best; it was a good collaborative effort."

Julia Ryan of Dunn & Associates, a design firm in Hayward, Wis., follows a similar process. "Initially, I ask a lot of questions: what the function of the book is, who is the target audience, where the book will be distributed, if they've done any pre-sales on it. We ask for one or two representative chapters, and a table of contents. If they are first-time publishers, we will spend more time educating them."

Anatomy of a Bookcover

The following may be 'Cover Design 101' for some of you, but it never hurts to touch on the basics. For book covers they are: the title, subtitle (if applicable), and author name on the front; a category listing, sales statement (including a headline), price and bar code with an ISBN on the back; and the title, author name and publisher on the spine. These basic components are like the foundation for a house: They are the beginnings, what you build on. And just as a farm house would look out of place in the middle of suburbia, a book needs to belong in its environment.

"When you have a book that's made for a bookstore, yes, it has to be different, but it can't be too different," says Linda Nathanson of Edin Books Inc., a small-press publisher in Gillette, N.J. "It has to look like it belongs in the category."

Ryan agrees. "There is a general schematic look to certain books," she says. "A business book needs to look different than a fiction book. You can still, however, do very unique and special designs for individual books because there is not a formula that has to be followed."

Typography

The choice of type, and how it will be used, is a key consideration in a cover's design. Sometimes it's the entire design. Such is the case with Pulitzer Prize-winning author Jane Smiley's last novel.

"It just says, 'MOO, a Novel by Jane Smiley,' and you can't miss it," says Robin Feld, store manager for Barnes & Noble in Deerfield, Ill. "Conversely, Ann Tyler's new book has sort of a non-descript cover, but her name gives it recognition."

A *Cover Design* Checklist

Judges of book design for the Publishers Marketing Association's annual Benjamin Franklin Awards rate 15 different design elements on a scale of one to 10. The following criteria apply, either in whole or in part, to cover design:

Overall reaction:
Rate your initial general reaction to the overall book design.

Appearance:
Is the cover design pleasing and interesting, and does it evoke a positive response? Do you want to pick up the book and examine it more closely?

Layout:
Does the organization of cover elements allow instantaneous "reading"?

Organization:
Do color choices stimulate interest and seem to fit with the subject matter?

Color:
Do color choices show good contrast or complement each other well?

Photographs and illustrations:
If used, are photographs or illustrations appropriate, of good quality and reproduced well?

Graphics:
Are type styles and overall graphic treatment easy to read and appropriate to the subject matter and intended audience?

Typography:
Are letterspacing, linespacing and wordspacing correct and pleasing to the eye?

Back, spine:
Does the back cover, spine and flap (if any) design inform easily and interestingly?

Front, spine:
Are front and spine copy legible from a reasonable distance, so as to show up on a bookstore shelf?

Essentials:
Are the publisher's name, logo and ISBN on the back cover or spine?

Most designers recommend using type sparingly. "The shorter the title and the descriptive copy, the easier it is to work with," says Aulincino. "How much are people going to read, anyway?"

Additional information about the book is best reserved for the back cover.

Color

A dilemma many small publishers face when budgeting for cover design is choosing a one-, two-, three- or four-color process. Four-color book covers are becoming commonplace primarily because they do demand attention.

"The book cover is not the area to be conservative," Ryan says. "This is the one visual that sells the book. You can have some gorgeous covers with one and two color; it just depends on what you do with it. Four-color does give more room to maneuver around in."

Goldstein, for one, believes the minimalist motto of 'less is often more'. "People look at four-color and they see this tremendous visual excitement, but there doesn't have to be as great a design concept behind it. With one-color, the design must carry it. Often it is a single color cover with a strong graphic that is very demanding."

Choice of color is unlimited – sort of. "Unfortunately, we work in a world of cliches," Ryan says, noting that some colors tend to be associated with certain book categories. "Right now, for example, many spiritual and religious books are using beautiful, soft colors, while the new age-type books have lots of purples and dark blues. There are exceptions to the rule, but you don't want to confuse the person who is picking it up."

Webster likes to leave his options open. "It all depends on the individual book and what you are trying to achieve with it," he says. "If I want colors to recede and fall back, I'll use a cool color. If I want colors to come forward and stand out, I'll use a warm or hot color. Then I'll start experimenting with colors and how they effect the colors I use around them. A color can be great in one combination and awful in another."

Aulincino recently redesigned a book cover for an author who had previously done his own design but felt that his book needed increased visibility. Aulincino chose gold, red, blue and black for the new cover. This made the book appear bigger, even though its size hadn't changed. "It looks like you're getting more for your money," he says.

Ultimately, Aulincino says, a book cover should have depth and dimen-

sion. "There's no reason a design should look flat. Even before the computer, there were ways to create a dimensional effect. Paintings aren't flat – why should a design be flat?"

Laura Pratt is the public relations director and "all around great gal" at Buckwilder Books of Williamsburg, Mich. She thinks the company has one of the best children's book covers out there for their title, Buckwilder's Small Fry Fishing Guide.

APPENDIX B

THE RIGHT ANGLE

How to find the news value in your business

BY NANCY MICHAELS

A few years ago, there was a cartoon in the *New Yorker* of a man watching a long, black limousine glide by. The caption said, "There but for the lack of media exposure go I."

Unfortunately, you'll need more than a few press clips before you're commuting to work in a chauffeured limo, but there is some truth in the bystander's remark. While positive press coverage does not guarantee fame and fortune, it does offer swift passage from obscurity to prominence. No other medium carries the weight of the independent press. Therefore, a news story about you or your company will influence people as nothing else can.

The question, then, is how do you grab some media coverage for yourself? It's easier than you may think. A good number of news stories are generated by outside sources, meaning, people like you and me.

As you start to mine your business for news stories, remember the difference between a paid advertisement and media publicity. If you want someone to buy your self-cleaning hydroponic turtle tank, you pitch its affordable price and state-of-the-art features. If you want someone to *cover* it, you reveal that you came up with the idea after a giant sea turtle rescued you from a shipwreck off the Cayman Islands. Of course, if you say this, it should be true. My point is that you have to figure out what the average person would find interesting about your business.

Seeing the potential stories in your business sometimes is simply a matter of looking at what you do from different angles. If you have trouble stepping back to gain this perspective, ask friends or colleagues to help. A brainstorming session may yield a number of ideas.

A story with news value usually contains one or more of the following elements:

Trend
Does the story tap into a social, political or economic trend? The media probably won't care about your restaurant's new children's menu, but they will be interested to hear about your innovative new Monday night baby-sitting service for patrons, especially if you pitch your business as an example of an evolving trend toward "family friendly" businesses.

Anti-Trend
On the flipside, has your business bucked a trend? A thriving privately owned pharmacy in a region dominated by chain drug stores is certainly newsworthy.

Human Interest
Do you, one of your employees, even a customer have an interesting story to tell? The expansion of a greeting card shop isn't likely to receive press attention unless the owner didn't learn to read or write until age 30. People make a story come alive. The best stories are injected with a human element.

Community Involvement
Do you use your position as a business owner to contribute to the community, preferably in a unique way? Nadine Snyder of the Anderson Agency in Ashland, Mass., donates 5 percent of her earnings to a local organization through her "Attitude of Gratitude" program. Because of this, Snyder has gained a reputation for being a giver and has had several articles written about her business in the local media.

Offbeat
Is there an unusual angle to your business? Can you find the humor or irony in what you do? A few years back, Oprah Winfrey did a beauty show about the restorative properties of Bag Balm, a Vermont-made salve that prevents chapped cow's udders. The segment was not only offbeat, it gave the makers of Bag Balm unparalleled publicity.

Significant
Are you doing something that affects people profoundly? A research lab may employ only a dozen or more people, but if it discovers a cure for cancer, you can bet it will make headlines.

Timely
Can you peg your story to a current event? A small furniture manufacturer appeared in the local news during the O.J. Simpson trial because Judge Lance Ito special-ordered his ergonomically correct chair from the company. Had Judge Ito ordered the chair six months after the trial, the editors probably wouldn't have written about it.

Prominence/Celebrity Endorsement
Can you link your service or product to a well-known person? If a court clerk ordered the chair for himself, it wouldn't be news. Having a celebrity for a customer gives the impression that you are in demand. You can encourage this perception by sending your product to local luminaries. Steve Latour of Washington, D.C., did this when he delivered his hand-made Hawaiian leis to local television weather forecasters during the blizzard of 1994. Latour got his plug when forecasters at the Fox affiliate appeared on air wearing his leis.

Superlative
Is your service or product the biggest? The smallest? The first? The last? It seems every summer there's a news story about drive-in movie theaters, simply because there are so few left.

Slice of Life
What may not have much inherent news value may find itself on the features pages as a slice-of-life story. These are the stories that put the reader into someone else's skin. For instance, a reporter may spend a hot August day in an ice-cream truck, then write about the vendor's experience.

Local
Do you do something that matters to people in your area? A gift shop grand opening in struggling downtown Jonesville isn't going to make it into the *New York Times*. However, it may very well appear in the *Jonesville Daily News*, especially if the opening is tied into a broader story about downtown revitalization.

Coming up with a Story Idea
Editors strive for a balance of news each day. The news you see in print and on air is a blend of entertainment, information and public service. The following suggestions will help you determine how you can fit into the balance.

Look beyond the business section
Just because you have a business doesn't necessarily mean you have a business story. Your idea may be more suited to the lifestyles pages, the local news section, even the sports pages.
See RIGHT ANGLE, *page 20*

THE RIGHT PEOPLE
Your story idea won't make it into print or on the air unless you get it to the right person. Here are ways to find out who covers what.
* Call the assignment editor and ask.
* Refer to a media directory. These list the names and titles of key people, such as editors and producers. They can be found in your local library.
* Study the publication or broadcast to determine the reporters' "beats" and to get an idea of the subjects they seem to favor. A general assignment reporter I know writes often about the outdoors, simply because the topic interests him. A wilderness trip operator would be most successful pitching his story idea to this particular reporter.
* Don't overlook professional journals and other industry-specific publications that your clients read. These list the quality, rather than the quantity of readers that is important. A *San Francisco Chronicle* story about your new medical management software would certainly be an ego boost, but you would probably sell more programs if the story appeared in a magazine such as *Physician's Management*.
* Remember your school alumni magazine. These are often read by a diverse audience and can lead to wider coverage.
* When you send your story idea, be sure to modify the message for each recipient. This means stressing the local angle of your story for the local paper, stressing the business angle for business journals, etc.

Before you drop your pitch in the mail, consider placing a very brief call to notify the recipient it is on the way. Again, make the call as brief as possible. Your primary purpose is to help your story idea stand out among the others when it arrives. In fact, if you can leave your message on voice mail, all the better.

A few days after your mailing was due to arrive, place another brief follow-up call. If your story idea is rejected, don't take it as a personal insult. Instead, ask for the names of others within the same news organization who may be interested. Also, send a follow-up letter thanking the reporter or editor for considering your idea. The next time that person needs a source for a story in your area of expertise, he may very well remember your professionalism, and call you for comment.

APPENDIX B   199

RIGHT ANGLE, *continued from page 17*
In fact, it may be to your advantage to appear in other, more widely read sections of the newspaper.

Think local
Don't underestimate the power of the local press. A good article in your town's newspaper can mushroom into a series of national news stories. After it appears locally, it may be picked up by a larger paper or news station, where it could be noticed by the networks. The media exposure could go on for months. This type of prolonged publicity is invaluable.

Stay informed
Not only about your industry, but about the world in general. If you can wrap your idea around a larger issue, you're more likely to have a winning story that includes mention of you. Jim and Amy Dacyczyn of Leeds, Maine, did this in 1990, when they promoted their newsletter, *The Tightwad Gazette* as a response to the economic recession. The press, always looking for new ways to write about the economy, seized on the story. The Dacyczyn's experience is also a good example of how a single story can blossom into national exposure. When the local newspaper ran an article about the newsletter, the story caught on nationally. *Parade* magazine, *The Today Show, Donahue, Wall Street Journal,* and most recently, *Prime Time Live* have all featured the Dacyczyns and their newsletter. Not only did circulation of the newsletter soar to 90,000, but the Dacyczyns were asked

to sign a book deal, and given the almost unthinkable advance of $250,000 for first-time authors. Now they have two best-sellers to their credit.

Be unconventional/innovative
Your spouse may not be crazy about this aspect of your personality, but the press loves a risk-taker, especially an outspoken one. If your opinion goes against conventional wisdom, your innovation turned around people's thinking or your contrary point of view brought you success, it may bring you publicity, too.

Be ready to pounce
The French novelist Andre Gide defined journalism as "everything that will be less interesting tomorrow than today." If you can link you or your business to breaking news, call the media – quick! If the Rolling Stones announce they're breaking up and a crowd of mourners dressed in black hold an impromptu vigil in the "R" section of your music store, pick up the phone! You can bet the next two people through your doors will be a news photographer and a reporter.

Peg your story to holidays, anniversaries and other widely recognized events
These offer ready-made news hooks for your story idea. In January, a florist may send the media tips for purchasing a Valentine's bouquet and suggest a story on the topic for Feb. 14. An allergist may want to contact the media during pollen season. If your endeavor doesn't fit into a well-known holiday, leaf

through *Chase's Calendar of Events,* which lists all sorts of little-known occasions that you might be able to link to your business. You can also invent your own holiday by submitting an application to *Chase's.*

Get published
You don't have to write a book, but if you come out with a position paper on a particular subject or even publish a newsletter, you will become regarded as an authority in your field. Think about the obligatory guest experts who appear on every talk show from *Oprah* to *Nightline.* What makes them experts are their publishing credits. Send copies of your published material to the media. Even newsletters get scanned by editors and producers for story ideas.

Publicity is a never-ending job. It's a way of life. Think about it all the time. Seize opportunities that pop up as you read the paper or watch television. Get yourself listed in the *Yearbook of Experts, Authorities & Spokespersons,* which is a directory of potential press contacts. Maintain a media file of special sections and segments where your ideas may fit in. If you have an interesting topic, a professional presentation and a good relationship with the media, you will make news.

Nancy Michaels is president of Impression Impact, a public relations and marketing firm based in Concord, Mass. She is also author of a two-cassette audio program, How to Be a Big Fish in Any Pond: Self-Marketing Strategies for Entrepreneurial Success.

BIBLIOGRAPHY

Bennett, Julie & John, Javna. *50 Simple Things You Can Do To Save The Earth.* Berkeley, Calif.: Earthworks, 1990.

Blanchard, Kenneth. *The One Minute Manager.* New York, New York: Berkeley Books, 1983.

Bolles, Richard Nelson. *The 1996 What Color Is Your Parachute?* Berkeley, Calif.: Ten Speed Press, 1996.

Brown, H. Jackson. *Life's Little Instruction Book.* Nashville, Tenn.: Rutledge Hill Press, 1991.

Canfield, Jack and Mark Victor Hansen. *Chicken Soup for the Soul.* Deerfield Beach, Fla.: Health Communications, 1995.

Cardoza, Avery. *The Complete Guide to Successful Publishing.* New York, New York: Cardoza Publishing, 1995.

Chopra, Deepak. *The Seven Spiritual Laws of Success.* San Rafael, Calif.: Amber-Allen Publishing and New World Library, 1994.

Chilton, David. *The Wealthy Barber.* Waterloo, Ontario, Canada: Prima Publishing, 1996.

Eadie, Betty J. *Embraced by the Light.* New York, New York: Bantam Books, 1994.

Eisenberg, Arlene, Heidi Murkoff, and Sandee Hathaway. *What To Expect When You're Expecting.* New York, New York: Workman Publishing,1988.

Evans, Richard Paul. *The Christmas Box.* New York, New York: Simon and Schuster, 1993.

Gallagher, Patricia C. *For All The Write Reasons.* Worcester, Penn: Young Sparrow Publishing, 1992.

Godek, Greg. *1,001 Ways To Be Romantic.* Weymouth, MA: Casablanca Press, 1991.

Hubbard, L. Ron. *Dianetics.* Los Angeles, Calif.: Bridge Publications, 1950.

Martz, Sandra Haldeman. *When I Am an Old Woman I Shall Wear Purple.* Watsonville, Calif.: Papier-Mache Press, 1987.

Morgan, Marlo. *Mutant Message Down Under.* New York, New York: HarperCollins Perennial, 1991.

Muir, John. *How To Keep Your Volkswagen Alive 25th Anniversary Edition.* Sante Fe, New Mexico: John Muir Publications, 1994.

Munsch, Robert. *Love You Forever.* Willowdale, Ontario, Canada: Firefly Books, 1986.

Naiman, Arthur. *The Macintosh Bible.* Berkely, Calif.: Peachpit Press, 1992.

Poynter, Dan. *The Self-Publishing Manual.* Santa Barbara, Calif. Para Publishing, 1996.

Redfield, James. *The Celestine Prophecy.* New York, New York: Warner Books, 1993.

Ross, Tom and Marilyn. *The Complete Guide To Self-Publishing.* Cincinnati, OH: Writer's Digest Books, 1994.

INDEX

50 Simple Things You Can Do To Save The Earth, 61

1001 Ways to be Romantic, 67

Advance, 166

Agent, 35, 36, 130, 149

American Booksellers Association, 68, 183

Bennett, Julie, 61

Blanchard, Ken, 139

Bolles, Richard Nelson, 153

Book reviews, 42, 46, 106, 117, 133, 135

Brown, H. Jackson, 75

Canfield, Jack, 49

Chicken Soup for the Soul, 49

Chilton, David, 101

Chopra, Deepak, 179

Contract, 35,

Costs, 68, 115

Cover design, 93

Dianetics, 83

Eadie, Betty, J., 161

Editing, 105, 136, 158

Eisenberg, Arlene, 123

Embraced by the Light, 161

Evans, Richard Paul, 31

Godek, Greg, 67

Hansen, Victor Mark, 49

Hathaway, Sandee Eisenberg, 123

How to Keep Your Volkswagen Alive, 169

Hubbard, L. Ron, 83

Inspiration, 33, 50, 103, 184

Legal, 148

Life's Little Instruction Book, 75

Martz, Sandra Haldeman, 111

Marketing, 33, 42, 51, 53, 63, 71, 106, 118, 148

Morgan, Marlo, 145

Munsch, Robert, 93

Muir, John, 169

Murkoff, Heidi Eisenberg, 123

Mutant Message Down Under, 145

Naiman, Arthur, 131

New York Times, 50, 55, 61, 64, 79, 84, 88, 94, 131, 143, 148, 150, 163, 180

People Weekly, 35, 43, 46, 51, 55

Profit, 105, 117, 120

Promotion, 55, 189

Printer, 45, 53
Publicity, 47, 55, 102, 147
Publishers Weekly, 31, 35, 46, 48,
	132, 148, 150, 180

Redfield, James, 41
Rejection, 35, 45

The Christmas Box, 31
The Celestine Prophecy, 41
The Macintosh Bible, 131
The One Minute Manager, 139
*The Seven Spiritual Laws of
	Success,* 179

The Wealthy Barber, 101

USA Today, 55, 79, 125

What Color Is Your Parachute, 153
*What To Expect When You're
	Expecting,* 123
*When I Am An Old Woman I Shall
	Wear Purple,* 111

MARDI LINK

ardi Link is executive editor of *Small Press* and
Publishing Entrepreneur magazines, two trade
publications which cover the independent pub-
lishing industry. She is a journalism graduate from
Michigan State University, a former reporter for *Fosters
Daily Democrat* in Dover, New Hampshire, and is current-
ly researching a second book on best-selling authors. She
lives in Traverse City, Michigan, with her husband Jay
Tomaszewski, a kindergarden teacher, their two sons,
Owen, 6, and Luke, 4, and a third child expected in 1997.